Sara Y. Aharon

FROM KABUL TO QUEENS

THE JEWS OF AFGHANISTAN AND
THEIR MOVE TO THE UNITED STATES

AMERICAN SEPHARDI FEDERATION
New York, NY

DECALOGUE BOOKS
Mount Vernon, NY

Published jointly in the United States by the

AMERICAN SEPHARDI FEDERATION
15 West 16th Street
New York, NY 10011
www.americansephardifederation.org
(212) 294-8350

and

DECALOGUE BOOKS
7 North MacQuesten Parkway
Mount Vernon, NY 10550
www.decaloguebooks.com
(914) 664-5930

Library of Congress Cataloging-in-Publication Data

Aharon, Sara Y., 2011.
From Kabul to Queens: The Jews of Afghanistan and Their Move to the United States / by Sara Y. Aharon.
p. cm.
Includes bibliographical references and index.
ISBN: 978-0-692-01070-9 (American Sephardi Federation)
ISBN: 978-0-915474-11-0 (Decalogue Books)
1. Jews—Afghanistan. 2. Afghanistan—Jewish history. 3. Afghan Jews—United States—20th century. 4. Afghanistan—history. I. Title.

Design: RitaLascaro.com

Dedicated, with love and gratitude, to my parents

Dr. Raphy and Joy Aharon

*who always encouraged me to become a writer
from the first time I wished it at age six.*

CONTENTS

ACKNOWLEDGMENTS

The American Sephardi Federation (ASF) at the Center for Jewish History in New York turned my dream of publishing this book into a reality. ASF believed in me and in this project from its very inception. My sincere appreciation goes to David E. R. Dangoor, president, and Stanley A. Urman, executive director. I was an editorial intern at ASF during the summer of 2007, when I had the opportunity to start my research in the library's archives. My deep gratitude goes to Lynne Winters, director of programming, for making it all happen, and for her guidance through the entire process. I thank both her and Ellen Cohen for their constant warmth and kindness, and faith in this book. They welcomed me into ASF, and I feel personally connected to the organization in a profound way. I appreciate that they are keeping alive the stories of Jews from around the globe.

My tremendous thanks to William Brandon, publisher, and to the staff of Decalogue Books. Bill steered the book toward its beautiful completion, focusing on every last detail down to the Index.

From Kabul to Queens: The Jews of Afghanistan and Their Move to the United States stemmed from my B.A. thesis at Brandeis University, which I researched and wrote during my senior year. I am indebted to my thesis advisor, Dr. Jonathan Sarna, an extraordinary professor and mentor. I thank him for his wisdom and constant support at all hours of the day and night. It was an honor to work under the tutelage of such an accomplished scholar who gave me the foundation to study history and the confidence to continue doing so.

The idea for my thesis partially originated from a paper I wrote for Dr. Sylvia Barack Fishman's class as a sophomore, when she encouraged me to research the religious identities of non-Ashkenazi Jews in the United States. Professor Fishman is a true teacher in every sense of the word, and a wonderful source of academic guidance. My gratitude goes to Professor Fishman for her time, advice, and encouragement.

I thank Dr. Joseph Lumbard for explaining Islam with thoroughness and enthusiasm, and Dr. Avigdor Levy, a scholar of Jews in Muslim lands and member of my thesis committee. I have taken and enjoyed classes with these esteemed Brandeis professors. They provided me with much necessary and vital background in Islamic religious and social history.

Thank you to the kind members and staff at the Center for Jewish History's library, the Central Zionist Archives in Jerusalem, and Congregation Anshei Shalom in Queens, New York for their invaluable research assistance.

I also extend much appreciation to Rosanne Klass, former New York Times correspondent on Afghanistan and author of *Land of the High Flags: Afghanistan When the Going Was Good.* Her lively first-hand stories gave me a rare perspective into Afghan life in the 1960s and 1970s when the country was arguably in its heyday, and truly her stories "could not be found in books." The documents in the Rosanne Klass Special Collection on Afghanistan at the Milton Eisenhower Library of Johns Hopkins University are an important resource for studying Afghan history.

My heartfelt gratitude goes to the numerous contributors who guided this book through its final stages, especially Rita Lascaro, my graphic designer and layout editor, and Eileen Maass, my copy editor. It was a pleasure to work with such talented and caring individuals.

The ten participants I interviewed for this book were tremendous assets in making the world of Afghan Jewry come alive. Their stories help to preserve Afghan history, and this book is richer because of their contributions and insights.

My friends from Brandeis University and elsewhere have been a firm support throughout this process, from the dorms to Sherman meals to our post-college adventures. Their excitement for this project and sympathy for the challenges of conducting research has been so valuable and continues to touch my heart.

—⁓—

My grandfather, Joseph Koreen, M.D., amazes me. He survived hardships in Baghdad to become a pediatrician, as well as the *baal koreh* [Torah reader] at his synagogue in New York. As many tell me, my grandmother, Grace Golda, of blessed memory, was a kind woman whose name described her sweet and generous nature. I deeply admire my grandfather's incredible perseverance in his many accomplishments, and his devotion to Judaism. I wish I had his remarkable memory. This book is for him because, as he famously says, "All Jews are originally from Baghdad."

My grandparents, Shoshana and Gavriel Aharon, endured life in Herat to successfully raise six children dedicated to Judaism. I am inspired by my grandfather's community leadership in his synagogue in New York, where he was the president and *baal koreh* for several decades. My grandmother's food keeps Afghan Jewish culture alive, and her grandchildren full to bursting. I was fortunate to have met my paternal great-grandparents, *Saba* Yashar and *Savta* Yocheved, my namesake. Both my grandparents' families lived in Afghanistan for over two hundred years until they moved to Israel and/or America. Their commitment to family first continues to be a central value for all of us.

I am blessed that my parents, Joy and Raphy Aharon, constantly encouraged me and my four younger siblings to fulfill our dreams and aspirations. People who believe in you provide the confidence and strength to move forward, no matter what happens. My siblings, Devora, Moshe, Yossi, and Golda, always bring the fun, laughter, and Apples to Apples. And so my biggest thank you goes to my parents, brothers, and sisters for all their love, support, and incredible enthusiasm.

FOREWORD

My family is a lively mixture of Jewish individuals hailing from Afghanistan, Iraq, Russia-Poland, and Canada. I grew up with valuable exposure to the diverse cultures of these countries and their Jewish communities. I thus have always felt that it is tremendously important for Jews—and people in general—from various places across the globe to try to learn about and connect with one another. I humbly hope that this book can offer a meaningful step in that direction.

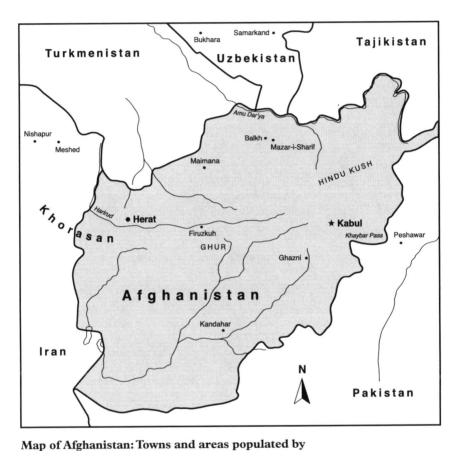

Map of Afghanistan: Towns and areas populated by Jews in Afghanistan and neighboring countries.

Map © The Israel Museum, Jerusalem, 1998. Courtesy of The Israel Museum.

Note on Geographical Terms

Afghanistan, whose Jewish population is the subject of this book, is sometimes described by the media as part of "Central Asia" and other times as part of "the Middle East." This double-label and resulting confusion arise because the distinction between the regions of Central Asia and the Middle East remains unclearly defined, even today. Many peoples native to Central Asia and especially, the Middle East, share Islam as a religion, but they are divided by language and other important cultural differences. The vast majority in the Middle East speak a dialect of Arabic—the language of the Quran, the holiest text in Islam—while peoples in Central Asia speak strains of Persian, Russian, and other languages. It should not be assumed, however, that language is the only significant disparity between Arabs in the Middle East and Persians in Central Asia; such a categorization would be overly simplistic. Arabs and Persians have separate historical narratives, literary achievements, etc. Yet for the sake of clarity, I consider and utilize language as a critical tool in distinguishing the Middle East and Central Asia from one another.

THE MIDDLE EAST: The term "the Middle East" seems to have first appeared in a 1900 article by a British general, Sir Thomas Edward Gordon, where he explained Britain's foreign policy interests. Gordon included "Persia and Afghanistan" as part of the Middle East.[1]

In the early 20th century, "the Middle East" was utilized to differentiate between "the Near East," which referred to the Ottoman Empire, and "the Far East," which included China. After the breakdown of the Ottoman Empire following World War I, the usage of "the Near East" faded and "the Middle East" came to encompass lands once part of the Ottoman Empire.[2]

Today, Middle Eastern countries are often called "Arab lands" because their residents' native tongue is Arabic. While numerous Arabic dialects exist, Arabic speakers are still unified by their shared usage of the language of the Quran.

In this book, I use "the Middle East" to refer only to Arabic-speaking countries, including those in North Africa, such as Egypt and Algeria. I thus exclude any non-Arabic speaking countries from "the Middle East."

CENTRAL ASIA: The region known as Central Asia, so-called because it encompasses many lands located literally in the middle of Asia, originally included Afghanistan and Iran, as well as the countries now known as Kazakhstan, Uzbekistan, Kyrgyzstan, Tajikistan, and Turkmenistan.[3]

Certain countries, such as Iran, have been considered as part of the Middle East or Central Asia. Iran sometimes appears on maps of the Middle East because it borders Iraq, but Iran also can be excluded from the region since Persian, not Arabic, is the main language spoken there. In cartography and especially, in colloquial speech today, "the Middle East" often includes Iran since it is simpler for the general public to understand world politics if Iran is considered part of the Middle East.

But I categorize Iran and Afghanistan, because they are both Persian-speaking countries, as part of Central Asia. Though occasionally Afghanistan is included on maps of the Middle East, today Afghanistan in its entirety is more often labeled as part of Central Asia.

Introduction

I vividly remember when, during one university guest lecture I gave about Afghan Jewish history, a tall, dark-haired woman in flowing pants raised her hand and introduced herself as the granddaughter of Herat's former mayor. She enthusiastically described to the audience her fond memories of the city's Jewish residents, including when they slaughtered animals according to Jewish tradition and "went separate from us [Muslims] to cut the chickens." She later approached me privately and thanked me for the presentation. I saw that she was happy to hear about a part of her country's history that did not revolve around September 11, 2001.[1]

On an emotional level, it was certainly thrilling to speak with the only non-Jewish Afghan I had ever met who still remembered a Jewish community in Afghanistan. From an academic perspective, her warm comments reflected the overall tolerance that Afghan Muslims and Jews enjoyed together over centuries, as well as the divergent perspectives that each held regarding their coexistence. For the most part, Afghanistan's Muslim rulers and populace felt at ease with the small Jewish community. In the 20th century, only about five to six thousand Jews lived in Afghanistan. Most resided in Herat or the Afghan capital, Kabul. The Muslims' relatively open attitudes toward the Jews differed considerably from the Jews' own wariness toward both their Muslim neighbors and the Afghan government. The Jews of Afghanistan never lost sight of their minuscule numbers or their vulnerability in a Muslim country filled with headstrong leaders, tribal conflicts, and rough terrain. Jewish men worked alongside Muslims in the public, professional sphere, but the community at large remained apprehensive about socially interacting with non-Jews. Afghan Jews rarely assumed that their safety was guaranteed. The Jewish community in Herat *voluntarily* segregated itself in one section of the city, creating a defined Jewish quarter.[2] Perhaps when the granddaughter of Herat's mayor said that the Jews would "separate" themselves to perform certain religious practices, she was referring to their departure from Herat's main area into this city's Jewish quarter. A private language also developed among Afghanistan's Jews. With Muslims they spoke the local Persian (Farsi), but among fellow Jews they conversed in Judeo-Persian, a mixture of Hebrew and Persian akin to Yiddish and Ladino. Afghan Jews' cautious approach toward Muslims, as we shall see, shaped their outlooks on many diverse elements in their lives from social mingling, of course, to education, folklore, and even architecture.

Before delving into Afghan Jewry's rich past, we must first understand Afghanistan's own history and place in the world. When studying Jewish history, or that of any minority, it is crucial to contextualize the community's experiences within the social and political circumstances of the majority population and of the country as a whole. This is especially true of Afghanistan, a land with a complicated past that is little understood or seldom taught about in the West. Afghanistan, located in the heart of Asia, is a landlocked country surrounded by Iran to the west, Turkmenistan and other areas once part of the former Soviet Union to the north, Pakistan to the east and south, and one arm of China to the northeast. Without exposure to a major waterway, Afghanistan suffered from a weak exchange of technology, materials, and intellectual ideas. Afghanistan's borders also were easily breached in all directions, as no natural water barrier provided a defense. Afghanistan was continuously invaded over the centuries, from Alexander the Great's incursions in 330 B.C.E., to Genghis Khan's assaults in 1222 C.E., and through modern times. The Anglo-Afghan Wars in the late 19th to early 20th centuries pitted Great Britain and Russia against each other in "the Great Game," as Rudyard Kipling famously called the conflict, to control Afghanistan and its routes to nearby India. Afghanistan finally achieved independence in 1919 with the close of the third and final Anglo-Afghan War, only to endure the Soviet invasion sixty years later. Learning about the constant attacks on Afghanistan aids our understanding of its peoples' deeply ingrained, fierce desire to be independent as well as their collective hostility toward foreign presences, sentiments that clearly remain in the early 21st century.

While many Afghans are unified in their resentment toward outsiders, they are conspicuously divided by ethnicity and religion into a multitude of different groups. The three largest populations living in Afghanistan are the Pashtuns, the Tajiks, and the Hazaras. The Pashtuns, as the biggest ethnic group, comprise about forty percent of the populace. Most Pashtuns reside near Kabul, Herat, and Kandahar. The Tajiks, the second largest group, account for approximately twenty-five percent of the population. The majority of Tajiks live in eastern Afghanistan, near Pakistan, though some reside in western Afghanistan. Both Pashtuns and Tajiks are Sunni Muslims. Meanwhile, the Hazaras, who comprise about twenty percent of the population, are Shiite Muslims. Their predominantly Asian features suggest that they descended from the Mongols. The Hazaras usually live in the mountainous regions of central Afghanistan, known as "Hazarajat." The two official languages of Afghanistan are Pashto, spoken by more than two-fifths of the total population, and Dari, the Afghan dialect of Persian. Though not all Afghans speak Dari, many speak some form of Persian.[3] Tensions arise not only between the above groups and others, particularly as the Hazaras are both an ethnic and religious minority, but also within each group and its tribes. Afghanistan is marked by its widespread tribal and patriarchal cultures, in which alliances are often based on blood relations.

Though many books about Afghanistan highlight its peoples' diverse backgrounds, the story of Afghan Jewry specifically is virtually absent in scholarship about Afghan history *and* general Jewish history.[4] The few sources that do discuss Afghan Jews focus on the time spent in their country of origin and on their later transition to Israel. Most of these books are written in Hebrew by Afghan Jews who moved to Israel themselves. At present, no scholarly works have studied Afghan Jews in the United States, where they have lived for over forty years. The researchers who mention Afghan

Jewry in America at all merely note that a large percentage of the community outside of Israel settled in New York.[5]

In an effort to help rectify this academic gap, *From Kabul to Queens* examines the history of Afghanistan's Jewish population together with its subsequent resettlement in the United States. I particularly explore Afghan Jews' shifting self-identities and the changing roles of their traditional Jewish institutions, like synagogues and Jewish schools, in these two countries.

The few existing chronicles of Afghan Jewish life, while quite valuable, almost exclusively emphasize the community's heavily traditional character and the Jews' tendencies to reject reforms.[6] It is true that the majority of the Jewish population in Afghanistan opposed modernity, fearing changes to its strict observance of Judaism. Afghan Jews "suffered geographical and cultural isolation from both the outside world and world Jewry,"[7] and thus were wary of secularization. But during the 20th century, Western ideals filtered into Afghanistan, including its Jewish communal institutions. A greater number of Afghan Jews, especially in the more modern capital city of Kabul, welcomed Western norms and secular education than previous studies have revealed. Openness to modernity in Afghanistan, though limited, would later aid Afghan Jews' acculturation to the United States. Upon arriving in America, they soon founded an Afghan synagogue in Queens, New York—Congregation Anshei Shalom—that sought to mesh traditional Afghan Jewish values with American democratic principles of governance.

From Kabul to Queens moves chronologically and combines historical and sociological approaches. Chapter 1 investigates the Jews' origins in Afghanistan, including their professed connection to the Ten Lost Tribes of Israel. I then describe Jewish settlement in Afghanistan from the medieval period through the 19th century. Chapter 2 details Jewish life in Afghanistan during the 20th century, highlighting the traditional functions of synagogues and other Jewish institutions, as well as the Jews' reactions to growing secularism in their community. Chapter 3 analyzes the causes behind Afghan Jewish emigration. Rising nationalism during the 1930s and 1940s prompted severe resentment of non-Muslims, especially in the economic sector. Discriminatory decrees against the Jews, who worked mostly in mercantile trade, led to their impoverishment. Even with such persecution, Afghan Jewry's emigration largely resulted from the widespread desire to move to the new State of Israel, rather than from discrimination forcing them out of Afghanistan. Chapter 4 explores Afghan Jews' adjustment to the United States and American norms, revealing that many of their experiences followed a typical pattern of acculturation that both Jewish and non-Jewish immigrants faced. As a particularly small (Jewish) population, Afghan Jews struggled to retain their religious and cultural heritage. Rather than continue to self-identify as "Jews from Afghanistan," where all were similarly observant, they began defining themselves in broader categories along American Jewish standards of ethnicity and religious observance. Once in the United States, Afghan Jews started to consider themselves "Sephardic" to distinguish themselves from the Ashkenazi [Central and Eastern European] American Jewish majority. Afghan Jews also began to newly identify as "Orthodox" in order to differentiate themselves from the Conservative and Reform movements, which originated in Europe and had no presence in Afghanistan or elsewhere in Central Asia.

Because few documents or studies exist about the Afghan Jewish community and especially its transition to the United States, oral testimonies played a vital part in illuminating the nuances of Afghan Jewish life. I conducted interviews with ten Jewish participants, seven men and three women, who all had personal connections with Afghanistan. For confidentiality reasons, their names are kept private. Of the ten participants, six lived in Afghanistan until their teenage years, when they emigrated. A seventh interviewee born in Afghanistan left at age two and grew up in Israel and the United States. I also conducted interviews with two college students, whom I call "youth interviewees." Only one had Afghan Jewish parentage, but both attended the Afghan synagogue in New York. The remaining interviewee was an Ashkenazi American Jew who traveled to Afghanistan en route to the Soviet Union in the 1970s and visited a Jewish family in Kabul. The interviews thus touched upon the last generation of Jews to grow up in Afghanistan, the generation born in Afghanistan but raised in America, the generation both born and raised in the United States, and an outsider's perspective of Afghanistan's Jewish community. In addition to their considerable contributions to this book, the interviews are important in and of themselves because they preserve oral histories of a rarely examined Jewish community.

I also note aspects of Iranian Jewish life in order to compare the Afghan and Iranian Jewish communities in both their countries of origin and the United States. The history of Afghan Jewry is intimately connected with Iran and its Jews. Afghanistan and Iran share a geographical border, across which people and customs flowed continuously over centuries. Although Afghan Jews and Iranian Jews came from similar religious backgrounds, they did not share an ethnic identity in either Central Asia or America.

This book does not focus on Afghan Jewry in Israel, a topic that certainly merits further research.[8] I am specifically concerned with the transference of Afghan Jewish life to the United States, and how Jewish institutions and Afghan Jews' unique identities altered.

Also, an Afghan Jewish folktale precedes each chapter to introduce its theme. These folktales provide a window into the world of Afghan Jews, thereby enabling us to better understand and internalize their concerns and values.

My humble hope is that *From Kabul to Queens: The Jews of Afghanistan and Their Move to the United States* may help encourage further studies of little-known Jewish populations from Central Asia, the Middle East, and from across the globe. By examining Jewish life in Afghanistan until the community's emigration in the 20th century, we will see what laid the groundwork behind the Afghan Jewish community in the United States. The adaptation and resulting identity shifts that Afghan Jews experienced in America have significant implications for other small Jewish populations similarly trying to acculturate *and* retain their distinctive traditions.

"The Princess Who Became a
Garland of Flowers"

Once there was a king and queen who had an only daughter. The queen died and the king remarried. The new queen was so cruel to the princess that she ran away from home. At last the princess arrived at a pool of water, but she did not know that this was an enchanted pool. Now all kinds of miracles were said to have happened there: a bird that had gone into the pool was said to have come out as an eagle, and a donkey was said to have come out as a stallion. The princess was so exhausted from her journey that she climbed a tree near the pool and fell asleep.

The next day a handsome prince went riding by the enchanted pool. He was astonished to see the princess's reflection in the water as she stared at him. They fell in love with each other at first sight and the princess agreed to be his bride. He told her that he would go to his family so that they could greet her with honor.

After the prince left, an ugly maid from a nearby town reached the pond, where she had been sent to fetch some water in an urn. Now this maid had a terrible temper, and did not know how hideous she was, for there were no mirrors in the land. When the maid came to the pool she saw the princess's reflection and thought it was her own. The maid cried, "If I am so attractive, why must I serve others?" And she broke the urn so that it shattered into many pieces. Twice more did the townspeople give her vessels to fill with water, and twice more did the maid break them when she saw the princess's reflection in the pool.

The princess had watched all that had taken place and said, "Why do you smash the vessels? That's not your reflection you see in the water—it's mine." The ugly maid was greatly startled. She saw her real reflection in the water for the first time. When she realized how hideous she was, she was filled with hatred for the beautiful princess sitting on the rock nearby and vowed to destroy her. The maid tricked the princess into giving her fancy dress and jewelry to the maid. Filled with loathing, the maid then pushed her into the pool. But as soon as the princess fell in, she turned into a stunning garland of flowers.

All of a sudden the prince returned. The maid, wearing the princess's clothes, pretended to be the prince's beloved. He was shocked that the beautiful girl he had left behind had become so revolting. But he was an honorable man and would stay true to his promise to marry her. As he helped her onto his horse, he was struck by the lovely garland of flowers in the pool. It reminded him of the beautiful princess he remembered, and he took it with him.

Now the maid saw how precious the flowers were to the prince and set out to ruin them. When the prince had gone, the maid tried to crush the flowers. But they immediately turned into a piece of parchment. So she tried to tear it, but the parchment was too tough. The angry maid then threw the parchment into the fire. When the prince came back, he found the parchment undamaged in the ashes of the fire. There was also a picture of the beautiful princess etched into the parchment by the flames. And the prince realized that the real princess must be under a spell, and that the maid before him was an impostor. His anger was so great that the maid confessed in fear, and the prince threw her into the dungeon.

Day after day, the prince stared at the parchment, wishing for his true love to return. Then one day he noticed something very strange. His room became mysteriously clean whenever he was absent. And the servants said it was already spotless when they came to do their own cleaning. The prince was so curious that he hid outside the door, and burst into the room when he heard sounds from within. And there was the beautiful princess, with a broom in hand, for she could leave the picture when the prince was not in the room. The prince, knowing something about the way enchantments worked, grabbed the parchment and threw it into the fire. This time it burned completely, and the spell was broken. The princess and prince joyfully embraced, and their wedding celebration was one of the greatest in all the land.[1]

1

ORIGINS

—⁊⁊⁊—

"The Princess Who Became a Garland of Flowers" uses fairytale imagery to describe a battle for a prince's affection between two women, one who is a true princess and the other, a deceitful maid. Considering the folktale's Afghan Jewish origins,[2] the princess probably symbolizes the Jewish people of Afghanistan while the maid, the impostor, represents the dominant Muslim population.[3] By highlighting that only the real princess will remain the ruler's beloved, the story invokes a powerful theme of Jewish survival. The prince symbolizes God, the ultimate monarch in the Jews' eyes. Regardless of the maid's numerous efforts to kill her, the princess lives to marry the prince in a glorious fashion. The unattractive maid's adornment of herself in the princess's clothes succeeds in deceiving the prince only for a limited time. "The Princess Who Became a Garland of Flowers" thus conveys that the Jews alone are God's chosen people even though others may "disguise" themselves as such. This folktale emphasizes that God always will be bound to the Jews who, much like the princess (and her altering forms), constantly adapt to survive adversity. The theme of a marriage between God and the Jewish nation found in certain interpretations of biblical and rabbinic literature[4] particularly enforces the folktale's representation of the prince as God and the princess as his everlasting Jewish bride.

This chapter explores the origins of the Afghan Jewish community and its development until the 20th century. Jews and Sunni Pashtuns in Afghanistan *both* believed that they descended from the Ten Lost Tribes of Israel who were dispersed in the 8th century

B.C.E. to lands outside of Judea. Though the legend of the Ten Lost Tribes traces the roots of the Afghan Jewish population to biblical times, the first epigraphical and literary evidence for an actual Jewish presence in Afghanistan dates from the Middle Ages. Following the medieval period, no scholarly records about Jews in Afghanistan came to light until the 19th century, when religious persecutions in Meshed, Iran forced hundreds of Jews to flee to Afghanistan. By delving into the pre-20th century past of Afghan Jews, we will see the foundations of certain values, such as the desire to be historically linked to the Holy Land, that continue to this day. While the Jews and the Sunni Pashtuns of Afghanistan shared certain communal legends and customs, Afghan Jewry, throughout the generations, always held firm to the conviction that God was tied foremost to his "true" bride, the Jewish people, even while they resided in a Muslim land.

THE LEGEND OF THE TEN LOST TRIBES OF ISRAEL

The story of the Ten Lost Tribes seeks to account for the disappearance of countless Jews during the First Temple period. After the fall of the northern Kingdom of Israel to Assyria in 722 B.C.E., ten of the twelve Jewish tribes were captured and banished to lands northeast of Judea, including Babylonia and Central Asia.[5] Biblical verses from Kings and Chronicles describe the Assyrian invasion and resettlement.[6] The tribes of Judah and Benjamin, who lived in the southern Kingdom of Judah, were spared from exile.

While many scholars hold that the Ten Lost Tribes assimilated out of existence,[7] some believers in the legend assert that they have located them, that modern-day communities descend from the lost Israelites, or that the tribes eventually will be discovered. Indian and Ethiopian Jews, for example, particularly identify with this story. The former refer to themselves as the *Bene Menashe*, the "Sons of (the tribe of) Manasseh [*sic*]."[8] Ethiopian Jews call themselves the *Beta Israel*, the "House of Israel,"[9] reflecting their professed ancestral connection with the lost Israelite tribes, rather than those of Judah. Some of today's leading rabbis in Israel consider Ethiopian Jews to be specifically from the tribe of Dan.[10]

This legend about the Ten Lost Tribes, surviving throughout the Middle Ages, remained vital to the Jewish identity of Central Asian Jews for centuries. The 12th century explorer Benjamin of Tudela described the enduring belief in the legend among Jewish communities in Central Asia during his journeys to a number of towns there.[11] He specifically mentioned Nisapur, a city close to Meshed, in eastern Iran. According to one 1900 translation of Benjamin's travelogue *Sefer Ha-massaot* [Book of Travels], Benjamin recorded that "Jews...who live in Persia at present report that the *cities* of Nisapur are inhabited by four tribes of Israel."[12] Meanwhile, a later 1905 translation of Benjamin's work stated that Jewish tribes resided "in the *mountains* of Nisabur [*sic*]."[13] Whether these tribes dwelled in cities or mountains affects the likelihood that Jews settled in such areas, but the true significance of the passage lies in Central Asian Jews' identification of their ancestors with the lost Israelites, specifically those of "the tribe of Dan, the tribe of Zebulun, the tribe of Asher, and the tribe of Naphtali."[14]

Though sparse information exists about Central Asian Jewry between the Middle Ages and the 20th century, certain accounts appear sporadically that convey the continued presence of the legend. In 1646, a *shaliah* [emissary of Zion] named Barukh Gad went from Jerusalem to visit the Jews in Iran, seeking to spread a love for the Holy Land and to request financial assistance for its Jewish community. His reports of "alleged meetings with the Ten Tribes" signify that the story was still prominent among Central Asian Jews, who seemed desirous to emphasize their connection with ancient Israel to foreign Jewish travelers.[15]

In the 19th century, another adventurer, Israel Joseph Benjamin (1818–1864), journeyed to the Middle East, Central Asia, and East Asia in search of the Ten Lost Tribes.[16] Also known as "Benjamin II," Israel Joseph Benjamin fashioned himself after Benjamin of Tudela in both act and name. Returning to Europe in 1851 via Iran, Benjamin II reported that the Jews there not only described themselves as the remnants of the lost tribes, but he fervidly agreed that the majority actually were so:

> All Jews in Persia declare unanimously that they are descendants of the first exiles from the kingdom of Israel. Although a small number belonging to the tribes of Judah and Benjamin are to be found among them, it is still without doubt that the greater number of them descend from the ten tribes . . . They date from the time of the First Temple, from the first centuries of the dispersion of the Jews.[17]

Although the accounts from the 12th, 17th, and 19th centuries do not necessarily indicate a continuous Jewish presence in Central Asia, it is significant that Jewish communities found there, across a span of 700 years, maintained the same communal myth. The legend solidly connected Central Asian Jewry with ancient Jewish history and the Land of Israel.[18] While enduring difficult situations in life, Central Asian Jews could cleave to the idea that they were keeping the descendants of the lost Israelites alive. Benjamin II emotionally expressed the predicaments of Jews living in countries untouched by "justice," "tolerance," and "equal rights," saying that "the children of the ten tribes of Israel scattered among the barbarous nations of the East continue to live in ignorance . . . unheeded and debased as Parias [sic] under the yoke of their oppressors."[19] Suffering in a remote region disconnected from much of world Jewry, the legend of the Ten Lost Tribes instilled Central Asian Jews with the hope of returning to a Jewish homeland and a nation that would provide and care for them.

While Benjamin II did not specify the myth's existence among Afghan Jewry, as he spent little time in Afghanistan due to safety reasons,[20] the Jews of Afghanistan shared and transmitted this legend for generations. Many Iranian Jews, as detailed later in this chapter, migrated to Afghanistan specifically during the 19th century and joined the Jewish community there. Fleeing religious persecution in Meshed, they brought their communal stories to their new homes in Afghanistan.

More surprising than the Afghan Jewish belief in the legend is that Sunni Pashtuns, the largest ethnic group in Afghanistan, *also* claimed that they, along with the Jews, descended from the Ten Lost Tribes. The 19th century Jewish explorer Ephraim Neumark reported in his journal *Masah Bi-eretz Ha-kedem* [Travel in the Eastern Land] that "the Afghans are Sunni Muslims, not Shiites, and from this they link their lineage with the tribe of Benjamin."[21] He described how Jews and Pashtuns in Afghanistan followed similar practices, such as refraining from eating milk and meat together, growing side curls, and wearing garments with fringes at the corners that "resemble *tzitzit*."[22] The Pashtuns, who even called themselves the *Bani Israil* [Children of Israel], also required their women to adhere to certain ritual purity laws; i.e., after menstruation, the women immersed themselves in water.[23] To Neumark, such identical customs revealed that Afghan Muslims were, indeed, from the "seed of the Jews."[24]

The legend probably stayed alive in the 19th century among both Afghan Jews and non-Jews in part because of overall warm relations they had with one another. Neumark is most amazed by the close interactions between Jews and Sunnis:

> Since I saw it with my own eyes, I will say that the Afghan hates the Persian [Iranian Shiite] and loves the Jew, links his ancestry and is merciful to him [the Jew] and thinks of him like a brother.[25]

It seems that such feelings of kinship for the Jews, particularly over the Shiites in Iran,[26] spurred the sharing of common practices and communal stories between the Sunni Pashtuns and the Jews in Afghanistan. Afghan Jewry's own belief in the legend of the Ten Lost Tribes was continually solidified by the surrounding Sunni majority and Iranian Jews moving to Afghanistan, for these groups held that they, too, descended from the lost Israelites.

Indeed, Afghan Jews today maintain that their ancestors came from the Lost Tribes of Israel. One interviewee asserted that Jews initially arrived in Afghanistan during the First Temple period, when Assyria dispersed the Ten Lost Tribes. He highlighted that many other Jews remained in Judea until the Roman destruction of the Second Temple during the first century C.E.:

> We are from *Bayit Rishon* [First Temple period], whereas . . . most of them [other Jews] are *Bayit Sheni* [Second Temple period]. They are from *Galut Rome* [the Roman Exile], we are from *Babylonian Galut* [the Babylonian Exile]. They are two distinct exiles.[27]

It surprised me that this interviewee mentioned the legend of the Ten Lost Tribes of his own volition. His words were not in response to a specific question, but brought into the conversation of his own accord. The interviewee, born in Afghanistan in 1943, added that Jews "have been in Afghanistan for 2,500 years; we were there when Alexander the Great passed by, waved to him probably."[28] Clearly, the story remains prevalent among Jews who embrace the idea that their ancestors lived in Afghanistan for millennia.

THE MEDIEVAL PERIOD
Epigraphical Evidence

Though Afghan Jews for centuries have traced their origins to the lost Israelite tribes, the earliest archaeological evidence for a Jewish presence in Afghanistan comes from the Middle Ages. Discoveries of multiple stone tablets in the 20th century indicate that a Jewish community settled in central Afghanistan during the medieval period. In 1946, an unknown traveler found a 12th century tombstone in Ghur, a mountainous region in central Afghanistan about halfway between Herat and Kabul. Ghur was once a main commercial and residential area under the ruling Ghurid dynasty (12th to early 13th centuries). The tombstone was written in the Judeo-Persian language with Hebrew letters, and dedicated "in the memory of the pious, old, and revered Elisha b. Moshe Joseph, on the 24th of *Tishri*," the first month of the Hebrew calendar.[29]

In 1956, researchers discovered another stone tablet in Ghur, specifically in the area of Tang-i Azao, about 125 miles east of Herat.[30] Although not a tombstone, the stone tablet was also written in Judeo-Persian with Hebrew characters. One scholar ascribed the tablet to 752–763 C.E.,[31] while another dated it to 1300 C.E.[32]

The later tremendous discovery of numerous headstones in Ghur further solidifies the presence of a medieval Jewish population there. From 1962 to 1963, Italian architect Andrea Bruno located over twenty tombstones in Firuzkuh, the capital of medieval Ghur under its Muslim leaders.[33] Bruno found the headstones near the Minaret of Jam, a colossal tower built in Firuzkuh between 1163 and 1203.[34] The minaret was about sixty meters high, and eight meters wide at the base. The Afghan government had requested that Bruno design protection for the minaret's base from water corrosion since the tower was located between two rivers, the Hari Rud and the Jam Rud.[35] Bruno identified the tablets as Jewish tombstones because of their Hebrew lettering.[36] The headstones' inscriptions, which scholars dated to 1115–1215 C.E., included words in Judeo-Persian, Hebrew, and in one case, even Aramaic.[37] Bruno hypothesized that rough weather elements, such as heavy rains and landslides, caused the headstones to fall from a Jewish cemetery on a mountaintop to the area near the minaret below.[38] The closeness of the tombstones to one another signifies that they once formed a Jewish cemetery in Firuzkuh[39] and that a Jewish community probably lived there or near this town.

The headstones around the Minaret of Jam, furthermore, may shed light on the length of time the Jewish community lived in central Afghanistan. Bruno wrote that ruins surrounding the minaret seemed like military fortifications, and suggested that an army camp or base might have been situated in Firuzkuh. Jews who settled near the fortifications may have conducted business with the camp for equipment, food, or other needs.[40] If we accept Bruno's proposition, then the medieval Jewish population in Ghur was likely an established community rather than a temporary one.[41] Such trade and commerce with the military site could have provided for the Jews' financial concerns, allowing them to remain in Firuzkuh for decades. The dating of the numerous tombstones near the Minaret of Jam, which span 100 years, particularly suggest that Jews in central Afghanistan resided there for a significant period of time.

Not only do the stone tablets show that Jewish communal life once existed—and perhaps thrived—in medieval Afghanistan, but the tablets' languages also reveal the origins of the Jews there. The consistent use of Judeo-Persian on the tablets indicates that Jews in medieval Afghanistan probably had Iranian ancestry. Plus, the Hebrew words on the Firuzkuh headstones suggest that the Jews utilized this language for important issues concerning the deceased. While Jews in Firuzkuh used Judeo-Persian to record nondescript words such as "day" and "year," they employed Hebrew to write the Jewish months, honorary titles like *tzadik* [righteous person] and *melamed* [learned person], and the names of the departed and his or her father. The Jews of Firuzkuh not only knew and could write Hebrew to some extent, but they reserved the language for matters distinctly related to Judaism.[42]

We further see the importance of Hebrew to medieval Afghan Jewry through the discovery of a tombstone in Kabul, dated to 1365 C.E., which contains an inscription written entirely in Hebrew. This dedication suggests that Hebrew became essential for marking Jewish headstones. Raised in memory of "Moses ben Ephraim Bezalel," the tombstone also reveals that at least some Jews in Kabul had distinctly Jewish names. While we cannot make generalizations based on a single headstone about Kabul's Jewish life in the 14th century, the all-Hebrew engraving does imply that Jews knew and used more Hebrew in cities, such as Kabul, than mountainous regions like Firuzkuh.[43]

Though the Jews in all areas of medieval Afghanistan spoke Persian and Judeo-Persian in everyday life, they held Hebrew as an integral part of their identity. They utilized the language connected to the Bible and the Holy Land to honor their brethren's final resting place.

Literary Evidence: Khorasan

In addition to archaeological evidence, Jewish and Muslim texts written between the 8th and 13th centuries point to a Jewish presence in medieval Afghanistan. In both Jewish and non-Jewish sources, Afghanistan was part of the region of Khorasan, a province or district that also included eastern Persia and Turkestan.[44] Though Khorasan's borders fluctuated,[45] areas in present-day Afghanistan continuously remained part of Khorasan.[46]

Rabbinic, Gaonic, and Karaite sources mention Khorasan as a dwelling place of the Jews.[47] The Gaonim of Babylonia, the center of early medieval Jewish life, seemed particularly concerned with keeping Khorasan under their financial and religious control. The 9th century chronicle of a Babylonian Jew named Natan Ha-bavli [Nathan the Babylonian] detailed a dispute between the exilarch—the leader and representative of the Babylonian Jewish community[48]—and the head of Pumbedita, a main yeshiva in medieval Babylonia, about monetary jurisdiction over the Jews in Khorasan.[49] Natan Ha-bavli's account was the first report of "Khorasan as an actual seat of Jewish community life in medieval Islam."[50] Khorasan also served as a place of exile for those who challenged Gaonic authority because of the region's distance and isolation from the Jewish community in Babylonia. *The Letters of Rabbi Sherirah Gaon* [*Iggereth R. Sherirah Gaon*] described how the Gaonim banished a Jewish individual to Khorasan in 933 C.E. after he opposed the exilarch Josiah Hassan.[51]

The Gaonim, furthermore, acted as Khorasan's *halakhic* [Jewish legal] authority, mandating that the Jews of Khorasan must follow religious practices set by the Babylonian rabbis. In the 10th century, Rabbi Judah Gaon sent a legal ruling from Babylonia to Khorasan's Jews to alter their customs regarding engagements to women. Instead of betrothing a woman with a ring and a feast, practices over a century old in Khorasan, Jews there were ordered to adhere to the Babylonian tradition, which required a marriage contract [*ketubbah*], the signatures of two witnesses, and a specific blessing formula in a betrothal.[52]

We also see that the Gaonim sought to impose their religious beliefs on the Jews of Khorasan, and Afghanistan in particular, from Saadiah Gaon's responsa to a rebellious thinker from the city of Balkh in northern Afghanistan. A discussion of Khorasan and Afghanistan would be incomplete without mention of the story of "Hiwi al Balkhi" [Hiwi the Balkhi, or Hiwi from Balkh], which is well-known even today among Afghan Jews.[53] In the 9th century, Hiwi published a "polemical work which contained over 200 criticisms of the Bible."[54] Saadia Gaon rebuked Hiwi's unconventional claims, including those stating that God is not omniscient and that the Bible recognizes the existence of multiple gods.[55] Saadiah Gaon probably condemned Hiwi's writings, in part, to prevent his "heretical" thinking from influencing other Jews around him. While the previously mentioned Gaonic texts did not discuss the size of Khorasan's Jewish population, they revealed Babylonia's ties to Jewish communities in Khorasan and to Afghanistan specifically. Khorasan's connection with Babylonia continued at least through the 12th century, for Benjamin of Tudela wrote that the Babylonian exilarchs' influence extended to the provinces of Khorasan.[56]

Muslim sources, moreover, point not only to the presence of a Jewish community in Khorasan, but a growing one. The 8th century decree of Muslim ruler Umar II to his governor of Khorasan "not to destroy any synagogues, but also not to . . . erect new ones"[57] shows that the Jews had a settled community there and likely wanted to expand their synagogue life. The 10th century geographer Muqadassi also recorded, "There are in Khorasan many Jews and only a few Christians."[58] These Muslim texts did not explicitly mention areas in Afghanistan, but neither did they exclude Afghan cities in discussions of a rising Jewish population.[59] While Gaonic sources addressed Khorasan as a remote, isolated region, albeit one they desired to influence, Muslim texts conveyed that the numbers of Jews in medieval Afghanistan, along with other areas in Khorasan, were increasing.

Umar II's prohibition against the construction of new synagogues formed part of a larger series of constraints on Jews living in the entire Muslim world, not just in Khorasan. His Pact of Umar, created in the 8th century, thereafter classified monotheistic peoples in Muslim lands as *dhimmi*s, a "protected" class of individuals whose status lay between that of Muslims and of polytheists.

*Dhimmi*s, including Jews and Christians, were permitted to observe their respective religions in exchange for adhering to certain restrictions and extra tax payments. For instance, *dhimmi*s were forbidden to carry weapons. They also had to wear different, distinctive clothing. *Dhimmi*s were further banned from building their own homes or houses of worship higher than those of Muslims and, as mentioned, from building new synagogues entirely.[60] Though these decrees applied in all Muslim-controlled areas, Umar II's explicit command to the governor of Khorasan not to construct new synagogues signifies that Jewish life there was likely flourishing.

The multiple Jewish and Muslim texts from the 8th century onward thus indicate that a Jewish community resided in Afghanistan prior to the 12th century, the period from which most of the archaeological evidence comes. Whether the community lasted continuously from the 8th through the 12th century is impossible to determine, but the literary evidence suggests that enough Jews settled in Khorasan, including Afghanistan, for the Gaonim to be concerned over the region's finances, religious practices, and beliefs. The ruling of Umar II to retain existing synagogues is particularly significant, conveying that the Jews were allowed to practice their religion so long as their numbers did not threaten Khorasan's Muslim populace. While none of these documents discuss the size of Khorasan's Jewish population, they show that a Jewish community might have lived in Afghanistan as early as 400 years before the majority of the headstones found in central Afghanistan were raised.

The Size of the Medieval Jewish Community

To discover the approximate number of Jews living in medieval Afghanistan, we turn to the writings of Moses Ibn Ezra, an 11th century Spanish poet and philosopher,[61] and to Benjamin of Tudela in his *Sefer Ha-massaot*. Their accounts appear to be the earliest known records concerning the size of Jewish populations in Afghan cities.[62] Moses Ibn Ezra wrote that 40,000 Jews went to Ghazni, a city in eastern Afghanistan that was the capital of the Ghaznavid Empire (977–1186 C.E.).[63]

Benjamin of Tudela's report of the number of Jews in certain Central Asian cities, meanwhile, is less clear. In *Sefer Ha-massaot*, Benjamin of Tudela described a Jewish community in "Ghazna, the great city that is next to the River Gozan."[64] One scholar of Benjamin's work wrote that "Ghazna" was Afghanistan's capital in the 12th century,[65] meaning that Benjamin likely was referring to the imperial city of Ghazni also mentioned by Moses Ibn Ezra. But the size of its Jewish population is heavily disputed by two translations of Benjamin's travelogue, where he says that the number of Jews living in Ghazna was "*pay elef* [*pay* thousand]." Each letter in the Hebrew alphabet has a corresponding numerical equivalent, and the Hebrew letter *pay* denotes "eighty." One translator claimed that *pay elef* meant "8,000 Jews,"[66] while another stated that *pay elef* signified "80,000 Israelites."[67] It is more likely that *pay elef* meant "80,000," since "8,000" could have been written as *het elef* [*het* thousand] because *het*, as the eighth letter in the Hebrew alphabet, corresponds to the number eight.

If Benjamin of Tudela meant 80,000 Jews, then the numbers he and Moses Ibn Ezra put forth are probably too high.[68] It is unclear if either author's account stems from his own observations or from hearsay.[69] Their estimates cannot be relied upon for an accurate representation of the Jewish community in Ghazni/Ghazna[70] or even Afghanistan as a whole. Still, Moses Ibn Ezra's and Benjamin of Tudela's reports reflect a perception among certain European Jews in the 11th and 12th centuries that their brethren in distant lands numbered in the tens of thousands.

The Community Destroyed

Whatever the size of the Afghan Jewish community in the Middle Ages, the Mongol invasion into Afghanistan in the 13th century decimated the Jewish population, along with many of Afghanistan's other inhabitants.[71] Led by Genghis Khan, the Mongols were "pagan, horse-riding tribes of the northeastern steppes of Central Asia"[72] who slaughtered Jews, Christians, and Muslims alike[73] from 1221–1222 C.E. The Mongols not only killed thousands of people, but also destroyed their infrastructure and irrigation systems.[74] Herat and Balkh in particular suffered tragic losses. Balkh surrendered as the Mongolian army approached, but Genghis Khan still commanded his troops to murder innocent civilians.[75] All residents of Herat were besieged for six months until the Mongols penetrated the city and gathered the people for a massacre that lasted seven days. When the Mongols returned to Herat to make sure no one else remained alive, they "found two thousand more victims to add to the stupefying pile of bodies."[76] Before the Mongol invasion, Balkh had been a center of Jewish life in Afghanistan,[77] but no known evidence points to a Jewish population in medieval Herat.

The epigraphical evidence from the tombstones in Firuzkuh sheds further light on its Jewish community's fate. The latest dating of these headstones is 1215 C.E., suggesting that the Jewish community vanished less than a decade later.[78] The devastation wrought by the Mongols also probably destroyed any records Afghan Jews might have preserved. The tombstone from Kabul, dated to 1365 C.E., indicates that some Jews either remained in Afghanistan after the invasion or journeyed there from other lands. But the headstone from Kabul was raised over a century after the Mongol attack; especially since only one tombstone was discovered, we cannot draw any conclusions from it regarding the Jewish community after 1222 C.E. Perhaps some Jews escaped the bloody assault, but it is extremely likely that the Mongols eradicated almost all Jewish life from Afghanistan.[79]

The 19th Century

There is a severe lack of information regarding the Jews in Afghanistan for almost 600 years following the Mongol invasion. A Jewish community certainly may have existed during that time, but its records have not surfaced. Our knowledge of the history of Afghan Jewry resumes in the 19th century, with an 1812 marriage contract [ketubbah] from Herat. This document testifies not only to the presence of Jews in that city, but also to their observance of traditional Jewish law. Herat eventually would become the Afghan city with the largest Jewish population, mainly due to Herat's proximity to the Afghan-Iranian border.[80]

The most significant event of the 19th century concerning the Afghan Jewish community occurred over twenty-five years later, with the flight of Iranian Jews to Afghanistan following forced conversions in Meshed. In the spring of 1839, Shiites in Meshed attacked their Jewish neighbors[81] after a certain Muslim declared that a Jewish woman mocked a Muslim celebratory custom.[82] Following this Muslim man's accusation and cry for vengeance in a local mosque, a mob "slew thirty-five of them [Jews], robbed and plundered their property, and the rest of them saved their lives, but not their property, by reciting the Mohammedan creed. Only a few of them preferred death to apostasy."[83] According to the above words of missionary Joseph Wolff, the first to describe the religious persecutions,[84] most Jews desired to preserve their lives by converting to Islam rather than sacrifice themselves as martyrs. The Jews came to call the tragic occurrences of 1839 the *Allahdad* [God has given], because the Muslims cried out this phrase as they rushed to attack.[85] In his memoir *Korot Zemanim* [Chronicles of Afghanistan [*sic*] Jewry 1857–1904], Mattatya Garji, a rabbi and survivor of the attacks, declared that "everyone was gathered in one mindset to destroy, kill, and eliminate all the Jews and plunder their property" [*li-hashmid, li-harog, li-abaid et qol ha-yehudim ushlalam lavoz*].[86] He took his words directly from the biblical Book of Esther, where the author(s) describe how the wicked Haman sought to decimate the Jews in Persia and their possessions.[87] The *Allahdad* wrought a heavy emotional toll on the Jews of Meshed, so much so that a leading rabbi compared the surrounding Muslims with the most infamous and evil Persian figure in Jewish tradition.

While Muslims forced Meshedi Jews to convert to Islam, many of them practiced Judaism secretly. These underground Jews, known as the *Jadidim* [new ones],[88] went to the local mosque but did not, for example, eat non-kosher meat.[89] They bought non-kosher items at the market and then disposed of their purchases, trying to covertly slaughter other animals in accordance with Jewish law.[90]

The Jews seemed alone in their plight to preserve their religion. Iranian political authorities did not intervene or punish those responsible for the *Allahdad*. As for the European Jewish community, the vast majority never even heard about or realized what had taken place.[91] Eventually, the Iranian leader, Muhammed Shah (1820–1848), officially allowed the Meshedi Jews to return to Judaism in 1843.[92] But the fanatic vigilance of Muslims in Meshed prevented the Jews from actually doing so. These Muslims believed that defection from Islam, even for a forced convert, was punishable by death. The religious leadership in Meshed, "the holiest city to the Shi'a in Iran," held more power over the functioning of the city than did political rulers in Tehran.[93] Meshedi Jewish life thus continued underground for about 100 years, with the threat of death hovering over any Jews who revealed their true faith.[94]

In the face of such danger, a number of Meshedi Jews managed to escape to neighboring Afghanistan. They settled in the towns of Kabul, Maimana, Kandahar, and especially Herat.[95] These Jews were quite concerned about maintaining their Judaism, refusing to sacrifice either their safety or their traditions. According to the testimony of *jadidi* Smad Aqa ben Yosef Dilmani, the Iranian Jews "who did not want to lose their religiosity fled, they and their families, to Afghanistan and Turkestan, and they still live there."[96] Garji similarly wrote that "the fearers of God's word" journeyed to Herat after the *Allahdad*.[97] The Jews who went to Herat refused to lead a "double-life," yearning to practice their faith both inside and outside their homes.[98] Considering that the *Allahdad* forced Jews to frequent Muslim mosques and non-kosher markets, Dilmani's and Garji's views probably accurately reflect that Meshedi Jews who were particularly anxious about their religious observance sought a better Jewish life in a different city.[99]

The new arrivals in Herat reinvigorated the existing Jewish population there.[100] Ephraim Neumark, a European Jewish traveler to Central Asia in the 19th century, said that Herat's Jewish community expanded fifteen times with the Meshedis' arrival. He wrote, "In the city of Herat, a twelve-day distance from Meshed, there are 300 Jewish households, most of them from the remnants of Meshed . . . When the Meshedis came there in 1840, there were twenty householders found there."[101] Bentzion Yehoshua Raz, a chronicler of Afghan Jewry, wrote that Neumark's "300 households" denoted approximately 1,500 people.[102] The Meshedi Jews, concerned with maintaining a high level of religious observance, bolstered the community with fresh enthusiasm for and dedication to Judaism.[103] These Meshedis were eager to exercise their newfound freedom to openly practice Jewish customs, which they could more readily perform among tolerant Sunni Muslims in Afghanistan than among Iran's Shiites.[104] The indigenous Herati Jewish population was quite pious, but the addition of over 1,000 Jews from Meshed spurred heightened attention to the Afghan Jewish community's faith.

But a war between Iran and Afghanistan in 1857 soon threatened the security of Herat's Jewish community.[105] That year, the Iranian army entered Herat and gained control of the city.[106] To garner favor with the Iranians, unknown residents of Herat made false allegations against the Jews, charging them with importing and selling nails, horseshoes, and gunpowder to aid Herati soldiers against Iran's forces.[107] The Iranian army arrested the entire Jewish population of Herat and kept them under siege for nine months.[108] The Iranian authorities then ordered the Jews to walk to a fortress outside Meshed called Baba Qodrot.[109] Mattatya Garji described the dangerous, torturous march:

> They shamed the Jews with false accusations . . . and put into the heart of the king to decree on us an exile to travel from this city and exile us to Meshed . . . There was snow and hail and cold and several souls died on the way from the great cold and lack of bread . . . And in the month of Adar, close to Purim, we arrived in the city of Meshed but they would not let us enter the city, but they put us in animal enclosures, in a fortress called Baba Qodrot . . . and we were subject to disgrace and shame . . . And we were there for two years . . . And in the month of Kislev in the year 5619 (1859) we traveled

from Meshed, and on Monday, the thirteenth of Tevet,
we entered Herat, each man to his place.[110]

The Jews suffered from severe hunger and disease during the
forced evacuation to Baba Qodrot and their subsequent deten-
tion there. As Garji correctly wrote, the Iranians released the Jews
in 1859 following a two-year imprisonment.[111] When the Jews
returned to Herat, the Sunni Afghan forces already were back in
control of the city and the Jewish community was relatively safe
once more.[112]

It is significant that the captured Jews in Baba Qodrot, whether
originally Herati or Meshedi, chose to return to Herat instead of
Meshed. The native Jewish population in Meshed was still in hiding, fearing for their lives if their Judaism should be revealed. The
painful events of 1857 seemed to cement the desire of the Meshedi
Jews in Herat to reside permanently in Afghanistan.

The influx of Meshedi Jews marked a turning point in the Afghan
Jewish community's development, as the Meshedis came to comprise the numerical majority of Herat's Jewish population. Having
twice fled across the Iranian border, the Meshedi Jews brought
their customs and dedication to Judaism with them. In particular, their sufferings likely influenced the fervid religious outlook of
what would become the 20th century Afghan Jewish community.

But the Meshedis did not completely connect with the indigenous Afghan Jewish community. Though they invigorated Jewish
life in Afghanistan, the Meshedis in Herat "kept to themselves—
apart . . . from the original local Jews."[113] The two groups "developed completely differentiated identities," wrote Hilda Nissimi, a
scholar of Meshedi Jewry.[114] The more severe communal trauma
for the Meshedis was the forced conversions in 1839, while the
greater ordeal for the Afghan Jews was the 1857 imprisonment in
Baba Qodrot.[115] The Meshedis in Afghanistan even spoke a different dialect. The native Afghan Jewish population spoke a form
of Judeo-Persian similar to Afghan Muslims' Persian dialect, while
the Meshedi Jews conversed in another strain of Persian called
"Giliki."[116] Eventually the Jewish communities in Afghanistan

became more cohesive, as Jews born in Afghanistan of Meshedi parents considered themselves Afghans rather than Iranians.

As we previously saw regarding the legend of the Ten Lost Tribes, certain Jews felt emotionally attached to Afghanistan because they held that their families had resided there for thousands of years. The different countries of origin among Afghan and Meshedi Jews remain in their respective consciousnesses, even today. When asked during our interview whether her family's history was connected to the *Allahdad*, one Afghan Jewish woman answered, "They're different; they're Meshedi. We're Afghan." Her husband explained that both his own and his wife's families had lived in Afghanistan for centuries, ever since they came to Herat from Qazvin, Iran in the mid-1700s. Indeed, Khorasan's ruler at that time, Nadir Shah (r.1736–1747), had implemented a massive relocation program for over 100,000 of his subjects, moving them to and from various cities in present-day Iran and Afghanistan.[117] The interviewee's husband reiterated that their families and many others "came before [1839] to Afghanistan. We are not part of that [Meshed's forced conversions]."[118] Though Afghan and Iranian Jews often shared similar religious practices, the two communities held—and would continue to maintain—separate and distinct identities in Afghanistan and elsewhere in the diaspora.

"A Treasure from Heaven"

Once there was a bumpkin who prayed to God to be sent a treasure from Heaven—that was the only kind he wanted!

One day, as he was walking through a field, he spied an earthenware jar, opened it, and found it to be full of gold and diamonds. What did he do? He covered it again and put it back, saying, "I want a treasure from Heaven, not from earth!"

He continued on his way, met a passerby, and said to him, "Do you see that jar over there? Take it, because it's full of gold and diamonds."

The [second] man went and picked up the jar—and in it was a snake. At once the man covered the mouth of the jar and thought, "That bumpkin is trying to kill me, because what person would give away a real treasure?"

He was so angry that he decided to pay the bumpkin back. And so he went to the bumpkin's house and climbed up onto the roof. It was noontime, and just then the bumpkin stepped out on his porch for a breath of fresh air. Seeing him, the man on the roof opened the jar and tried shaking the snake down on the bumpkin. Instead, however, a shower of coins and precious stones rained down the bumpkin's head.

"Did you see that?" cried the bumpkin to his wife. "I've always wanted a treasure from Heaven and now I've gotten it."[1]

2

JEWISH LIFE IN
20TH CENTURY AFGHANISTAN

—ⱳ—

"A Treasure from Heaven" conveys the significance of seeking God over material objects. The main character, the simple bumpkin, essentially desires a divine miracle when he cries for a "treasure from Heaven." He scorns the easy discovery of jewels in a jar. It is precisely because he wanted a divine act that the bumpkin is the only one who then merits finding precious stones; upon recommending the jar to another, who then *expects* to attain diamonds and gold, the second man finds a snake inside. Startled and angry, he releases the snake onto the well-intentioned bumpkin. But the serpent, as it falls near the bumpkin's head, turns into jewels and coins.[2] The bumpkin's happiness comes after God saves his life, the true miracle, rather than after only receiving wealth. As the bumpkin yearned for divine intervention, it was his piety, unlike his neighbor's vengeful nature, that led to God sparing his life and granting him tremendous riches. The folktale underscores that devotion to the Divine, rather than the search for affluence, will lead to good fortune—both literally and figuratively.

The story reflects the strong religious character, and the importance placed upon God's care, which defined the Jewish community in Afghanistan for generations. Afghan Jews observed Judaism strictly; there were almost no known intermarriages or other significant deviations from traditional Jewish practices. While they lived in relative peace with the Sunni Muslims, the Jews, for the most part, always remained wary of non-Jews and of secularism in general. Yet within the communal majority's steadfast adherence to religious Judaism, modernity from both inside and outside

Afghanistan began to slowly affect the 20th century Jewish community. This chapter explores the causes behind this modernity and the extent of certain changes, such as advances in secular education, that entered Afghan Jewry's world.

POLITICAL AND SOCIAL ENVIRONMENTS
A Brief History of Kings

In the beginning of the 20th century, several Afghan leaders tried to introduce modern ideas into the country. Under the reign of Habibollah Khan (r. 1901–1919), Western fashion styles influenced the manner of the Afghan royal court and the elite classes. In 1923, the new ruler, Amanullah (r. 1919–1929), attempted to introduce major reforms, including coeducational schools and the unveiling of women, via a new constitution. But such moves angered Muslim conservatives, who drove him from his throne. Muhammed Nadir Shah (r. 1929–1933) formulated a more conservative constitution in 1931 to please his Muslim co-religionists, yet one still based upon Amanullah's reforms. Under Nadir Shah, the economy grew as small businesses developed. His assassination led to the reign of his son, Muhammed Zahir Shah (r. 1933–1973), whose openness toward democracy was greater than that of his predecessors. In 1964, Zahir Shah and his staff implemented a new constitution calling for a House of the People with over 200 elected members and a House of the Elders with over eighty members, "one-third elected by the people, one-third appointed by the king, and one-third elected indirectly by new provincial assemblies." Under his rule, women were allowed to be unveiled; he also approved the elimination of *purdah* [the seclusion of women from public view], "which theoretically increased the labour force by about half." A coup in 1973 ended Muhammed Zahir Shah's reign and paved the way for Afghanistan's entanglement with the Soviet Union, the *mujahideen* [native Afghan fighters], and eventually, the Taliban. Afghanistan's political history reveals not only the gradual influence of Western values in the country, but the vehement opposition to them in certain Muslim religious circles.[3]

Our concern lies primarily with the way such changes affected the Jewish community. I frequently refer to two years that significantly impacted the Afghan Jewish population: 1948, when the State of Israel was founded, and 1964, when Muhammed Zahir Shah introduced his new constitution. Although Jews in Afghanistan remained observant, they were not immune to the modernity filtering into their community and their country as a whole. Whether in opposition to or in support of progressive ideas, members of the Afghan Jewish community were sensitive to the growing presence of Westernization.

The Size of the Jewish Community in Afghanistan

The *American Jewish Year Book* (*AJYB*) provides the earliest estimates of the number of Jews in Afghanistan during the 20th century, but these early figures are questionable. Between 1916 and 1930, *AJYB* wrote that over 18,000 Jews resided in Afghanistan, an estimate that was almost certainly too high.[4] *AJYB* then more accurately recorded that about 5,000 Jews lived in Afghanistan between 1931 and 1961.[5] According to *AJYB*, the Afghan Jewish population decreased sharply in 1962 to only 1,000 individuals, and the community remained approximately this size through 1965.[6]

Afghan Jews themselves concur that there were about five to six thousand Jews in Afghanistan for most of the 20th century. One Afghan Jewish interviewee who emigrated in 1956 said that Afghanistan had a population of 6,000 Jews, around "5,000 in Herat and 1,000 in Kabul." Researchers for Jewish studies journals also recorded that there were 2,500 Jews in Herat alone in 1942,[7] and a total of 4,500 to 5,000 Afghan Jews in 1953.[8] We may safely conclude, therefore, that about 5,000 Jews lived in Afghanistan until the 1960s, when Jewish emigration from the country peaked.[9]

While *AJYB* originally overestimated the number of Jews in Afghanistan during the early decades of the 20th century, *AJYB* underestimated the size of the Iranian Jewish population. In 1916, *AJYB* reported that Iran had 49,500 Jews,[10] but other sources recorded as many as 75,000 during that time.[11] *AJYB* in 1947 stated that 50,000 Jews resided in Iran,[12] while one researcher, Hayyim J. Cohen, reported literally double that figure.[13] Meshed alone in 1948 had 2,500 Jews.[14] By 1950, *AJYB* recorded the more correct figure of 90,000 Jews in Iran.[15] In stark contrast to Afghanistan, Iran's Jewish population numbered around 100,000 for much of the 20th century until many fled after the Iranian Revolution of 1979.

A Traditional, Patriarchal Society

Despite the huge disparity in the relative sizes of the Afghan and Iranian Jewish communities, Jews in Afghanistan and Meshed shared a strong emphasis on religious Judaism. In interviews conducted with Jews born and raised in Afghanistan, participants from both Herat and Kabul noted the high level of traditional observance. One man from Herat said, "In Afghanistan, one hundred percent" of the Jewish community observed the Sabbath and kept kosher.[16] An interviewee from Kabul repeatedly stressed that Afghan Jews had "a fear of Heaven [God]." He added, "Nobody cooked" or "went to work" on the Sabbath.[17] The Jewish holidays, in particular, were strictly followed in Afghanistan. Women started cleaning two months prior to Passover to eliminate any scrap of leavened bread. Before the High Holidays, men brought sheep home to slaughter; their wives cleaned the meat in a process termed *nikur*.[18] Though it is difficult to be sure of the Jewish practices of the Meshedis because they had to hide their Judaism until the mid-20th century,[19] it is likely that many religious customs were the same in Meshed and Afghanistan. One interviewee from Kabul stated that the traditions of the Jews in Kabul came from Herat, and the "*Heratim* got it [many of their customs] from the *Meshedim*."[20]

A significant difference, however, between the Jews in Meshed and Herat lay in their respective intermarriage rates. Though religious practices were once strong in Meshed, the high level of commitment to traditional Judaism faded among Jewish children there. The years of covert Judaism took its toll on each succeeding generation of Meshedi Jews, who could not envision a time when Jewish customs were practiced openly. Younger Meshedis started "to disregard the traditions of their fathers, to marry Muslim girls and to reveal a strong tendency to assimilation."[21] In contrast, intermarriage almost never occurred throughout the entire course of the Jews' tenure in Afghanistan.[22] One female visitor to Kabul in 1966, two years after Zahir Shah introduced modern laws into the nation, remarked that "there was only one case in this generation" of a marriage between an Afghan Jew and a Muslim—and in that instance, the Muslim boy's family had kidnapped the Jewish girl.[23] Even with a more liberated society in the 1960s, intermarriage barely affected the Jews in Afghanistan. While it is unlikely that the majority of Meshed's Jews intermarried, they faced a serious challenge nearly completely unknown to the Afghan Jewish community.

Afghan Jews' religious observance was facilitated by their close living quarters within certain towns. Herati Jews voluntarily lived in one part of the city and essentially established a Jewish quarter, where they built their synagogues.[24] Jewish women in Herat almost always remained within the Jewish quarter,[25] just as most Muslim women stayed near their own homes. Buildings in the Jewish quarter surrounded large courtyards that had areas in the center for cooking and doing laundry. Several families resided in each building, which contained multiple floors. Kabul's Jews, meanwhile, did not live in a specific enclave, but in homes lining city streets. The modern atmosphere of Afghanistan's capital allowed the Jews of Kabul to feel more comfortable living among their Muslim neighbors than did Herati Jews. In both cities, the Jews' proximity to one another allowed for an easy sharing of traditional practices.[26]

Afghan Jewish life was especially marked by the absorption of patriarchal values from the surrounding Muslim culture. The Jewish community was organized by clans, similar to the tribal system of Afghan Muslims. Researcher Erich Brauer wrote in the early 1940s that "in Herat, the 2,500 Jews are divided into twenty families."[27] The leaders of the ten most influential families formed the *hevra*, an internal Jewish body that governed the community's private affairs. The *hevra* judged disputes in criminal and civil cases, using "fines and corporal punishments" to settle matters such as inheritance. They exercised complete autonomy over the inner workings of their community, as many Jews avoided the Muslim civil courts. The *hevra* also punished transgressions of the Sabbath and other religious precepts. For matters regarding marriage and divorce, Jews went to the *beit din*, or rabbinic court. Members of the *hevra* were responsible for burying the dead and helping the poor.[28] Additionally, the *hevra* elected a *kolontar*, a representative of the Jews to the government.[29]

We further see the patriarchal nature of the Afghan Jewish community through the role of women, particularly in marriage rites. Afghanistan's peoples, Muslims and Jews alike, viewed marriage primarily as a business affair. In the Jewish community, an intermediary conveyed messages between the families, as the bridegroom was not allowed to see his bride before the wedding. Once the bride's family accepted the betrothal, the two families celebrated together with a feast, where men and women sat in separate rooms. The men sang and danced, but the women could not sing while men who were not family members visited.[30] The prohibition against women and men singing together may have stemmed from Jewish religious injunctions, Muslim societal influences, or both.[31]

Ritual purity also played a significant role in the Jewish marriage ceremony. Days before the wedding, the women of the bride's family questioned her menstrual state to determine whether the ceremony could take place. After the wedding, the couple did not consummate their marriage "earlier than the third night," for it was "considered unseemly for the bridegroom to sleep with his bride the first night." The husband's dominant role in the marriage, moreover, was explicitly conveyed in the wedding ceremony, when the bridegroom approached his bride and stepped "lightly on her right foot to signify her subjection."[32]

Divorce, while allowed in Jewish law, rarely occurred among Afghan Jews.[33] An unhappily married Jewish woman was expected to suffer her lot in silence.[34] It is important to note that in rabbinic Judaism, divorce was considered disadvantageous for women; a divorcée, with no husband to provide for her, would have to return (with her children) to her parents' home as a financial burden. It is a modern concept that divorce could be beneficial for women, for that view assumes that they could monetarily support themselves. Before 1964, women in Afghanistan depended upon their husbands for a livelihood. Only after the new constitution's creation could more women uncover their faces and work in shops.[35] The opposition of Afghan rabbis to granting divorces likely stemmed from a desire to prevent the social embarrassment that divorce would cause the husband, but they also might have been concerned about the woman's fate.

Yet certain Jewish customs differed from those of Afghan Muslims, signifying that somewhat more progressive practices existed within the Jewish community at least by the mid-20th century. All Afghan women had to wear the *hador* [veil] masking their faces when outside the house,[36] but Jewish women, when inside the Jewish quarter, wore head scarves that left their faces uncovered.[37] A Muslim bridegroom, furthermore, literally had to pay for his bride, while Jewish fathers were responsible for preparing full dowries, including household items, for their daughters. In the 1940s, Brauer remarked, "In contrast to the universal oriental custom, which prevails among the Muslim Afghans as well, the Jewish bride is not 'bought' by the bridegroom."[38] Though including dowries was more often a European practice,[39] Afghan Jews provided them for brides. Because divorce almost never happened among Jews in Afghanistan, we do not know whether divorced Jewish women kept the items in their dowries. But the very involvement of a dowry—since it deviated from the general Afghan practice of setting a "price" for the bride—did not as strongly contribute to the idea that a wife was her husband's property.

Divorce itself, moreover, might have become slightly more of an accepted practice in the Jewish community, at least on an individual level. In his unpublished memoir written in 1987, one Afghan Jewish man recorded a fascinating and heartbreaking incident in the 1950s when he wanted his daughter, Shira,* to divorce her abusive husband, Yaakov* (the symbol * denotes that the names of the parties involved have been changed for privacy and confidentiality reasons). Yaakov also happened to be Shira's first cousin on her father's side. The author said that he was out of town on business when the family held the wedding, without his knowledge, in Herat. In his memoir, he excoriated his sister, Hanna,* Yaakov's mother, who had arranged the ceremony. The following is a translated excerpt from the memoir, which the author wrote in Hebrew using Judeo-Persian letters. The parentheses [ ] denote comments I added for clarification.

> They couldn't find a wife for Yaakov* [Hanna's son, and the author's nephew]. In the end, Hanna* [the author's sister] and Mother and my brother asked Shira* [the author's daughter] for Yaakov, but Yaakov didn't want. When I left Herat, I said to my wife, "Give Shira to Yaakov. Why shouldn't he want [her]?" I was not in Herat [for the wedding]. They made a forgery as if they asked my daughter from me . . . Where did I agree? . . . In the end, in the year *Tav, Shin, Yud, Aleph,* [1950/1951] they made the *huppah* [marriage ceremony]. I also was not at the *huppah*. After . . . at night, Yaakov threw the poor girl outdoors from the room. All this they hid from me. . . . Maybe 25 years, Yaakov left Shira as a . . . husband, but he held her to be a slave in her house, to work harsh labor [*avodot parekh*],[40] suffering, and all other work in the house. After a few years [after the wedding], I went to Hanna. I asked her if he [Yaakov] did not want to give her [Shira] a *get* [writ of Jewish divorce]. She said, "Maybe it [the marriage] will be okay." Also, Shira did not agree to receive a *get* . . . They [Shira and Yaakov] are still not settled, and also Shira suffers a suffering of death. And also I suffer all my life; all of the troubles I suffer, I suffered from Hanna. I do not absolve her and I do not forgive her in life or in death. I do not want her at my funeral or to mourn me . . . Yaakov, the son of Hannah, made me many, many troubles and pains. My poor daughter, Shira, suffered suffering for 37 years from him . . . He did not want; he will not want to give her a *get* and finish the matter.[41]

While it appears that the author initially had granted the betrothal of his daughter, he apparently did not formally approve of the match, since he declared the proceedings, "A forgery . . . Where did I agree?" He was furious that the *huppah*, the wedding ceremony, was performed without his consent and especially, without his presence. This incident alone shows some subversion regarding the father's position as the head of the family. Then he heavily directed his ire toward his son-in-law's abuse of his daughter and the original concealment of this cruel treatment. The author vividly depicted how his son-in-law "held her to be a slave in her house, to work harsh labor [*avodot parekh*]." This phrase *avodot parekh* is used in Exodus 1 to describe the ruthless physical labor of the Israelite slaves in Egypt; the author's comparison of *avodot parekh* to his daughter's misery shows the depth of his pain at watching his child in distress. He cried, "My poor daughter suffers a suffering of death." His anger over the marriage, then, stemmed not just at the secret manner in which the wedding was conducted, but more so because the match led to his daughter's physical and emotional agony.

What is particularly telling about this story is the author's demand for his daughter to receive a Jewish divorce once he becomes aware of the abuse she endured, even while she herself protested against a divorce and ultimately stayed married. It appears that he was the only party involved who desired the dissolution of the marriage. His sister, the groom's mother, also opposed a divorce, and the groom almost certainly did, as well. It is crucial to emphasize that the author was part of a tiny minority of Afghans, whether Jewish or not, who viewed divorce as potentially beneficial to women. Afghanistan was (and still remains) an extremely traditional society. We cannot assume that ideas regarding women's rights in Afghanistan became widespread or even accepted, especially before the new national constitution of 1964. Though women were not the purchased property of Jewish men, wives were expected to stay with their husbands. Nevertheless, a more modern concept of divorce influenced invidual members of the Jewish community by the 1950s, for the author actively sought a divorce for his daughter despite her own belief that she would be in a worse state of affairs without a husband.

Exposure to modernity stemmed partially from Afghan Jewish men's constant traveling for business reasons. Jews, and especially Hindus, dominated Afghanistan's economic sector. These non-Muslim populations were free from Islamic law's prohibitions against interest and usury, and so Jews and Hindus in Afghanistan could work more unrestrictedly than Muslims in mercantile trade, banking, and finance.[42] Afghan Jews' livelihood depended almost exclusively upon trade, such as exporting and importing goods like karakuls (Persian lambskins), carpets, textiles, and spare parts. They did not engage in agriculture or artisan crafts, such as builders', cobblers', and peddlers' work. Some Jewish men journeyed as far as England, Russia, and India to trade in furs and hides.[43]

More commonly, continuous movement occurred between Afghanistan, Iran, and Bukhara for commercial purposes. As early as 1914, London's *The Jewish Chronicle* reported that Russian Jews were moving to Afghanistan.[44] In the 1920s and 1930s, hundreds of Bukharian and Soviet Jews fleeing Bolshevism settled in Afghanistan.[45] One reason Afghan Jews traveled to Iran was to purchase decorative pieces for Torah scrolls, for they were not goldsmiths and relied upon metal work made outside Afghanistan.[46] Residents of Meshed, Herat, and Bukhara journeyed among these cities for mercantile reasons and to visit relatives. One interviewee described his own background as an example of the close economic and familial ties among Jews in these three specific locales:

> My father is Afghan, my mother is Bukharian. Bukhara, Herat, and Meshed—they are three sister cities. They were always, always, always connected. Jews traveling in-between the three. Because they were merchants; they would go from town to town to town. They got married.[47]

Like this interviewee's father, some Afghan Jewish men met their future wives outside Afghanistan while traveling for business. It seems that such couples often lived in the husband's country of origin; the interviewee's parents returned to Afghanistan, where his father was born and raised.

In the same memoir discussed earlier in this chapter, the author described his journeys to distant areas within Afghanistan. He did not indicate whether he also went as far as England or India, but he detailed his travels to the town of Maimana in northern Afghanistan. Afghan Jews regularly conducted trade through Maimana because of its proximity to Bukhara. In the medieval period, the government of Khorasan called Maimana, "*El Yehudia* [The Jewish Area]," testifying to Jewish settlement there. It is unclear whether the name change to "Maimana" resulted from the vanishing of its Jewish community or from a conscious effort by Muslim authorities to end the association of the town with Jews.[48] We know that in the 20th century, Jewish men set up a "merchant colony" in Maimana,[49] complete with a synagogue, ritual slaughterer, and multiple shops.[50] Some men would stay there for months or years at a time before returning home to Herat or Kabul. As a crossing for Afghan, Iranian, and Bukharian Jews, Maimana served as an opportune place to exchange merchandise as well as ideas. Between journeys to distant cities and the arrival of Soviet Jews, modernity began to touch the men, in particular, of Afghanistan's Jewish population.

SYNAGOGUES

With many Afghan Jews traveling frequently for business, the synagogue became the anchor of Jewish life for those who stayed at home. The synagogue, or *kenisa* in Judeo-Persian, "served as their spiritual center" in everyday life as well as for celebrating special occasions.[51] All synagogues in Afghanistan conducted three daily services in the *nusah*, or prayer version, called *Edot Ha-mizrah* [Middle Eastern Jewish communities], the *nusah* most commonly used in the Middle East—and still the dominant prayer version there today. Prayer books usually came to Afghanistan from Jerusalem via the mail.[52] Weddings also were conducted in synagogues.[53] Whether for worship or non-prayer related events, the hub of traditional Jewish activities centered upon the synagogue.

Both Herat and Kabul had multiple houses of worship. Herat was home to four large synagogues as early as the 19th century.[54] In the beginning of the 20th century, the Herati Jewish community built smaller attachments onto each synagogue where men would pray during the weekdays.[55] Sometimes on the Sabbath, when the community prayed in the synagogue's main sanctuary, individual families conducted memorial ceremonies for the deceased in these extra rooms. The construction of new additions to the synagogues testifies to the growth of Herat's Jewish community and its need for more prayer space.[56]

For most of the 20th century, Kabul had three prayer quorums. Unlike in Herat, Jews in Kabul held their prayer services inside the homes of specific families. One quorum was for Heratis, another for Bukharians, and the third for Jews from Balkh. Although the quorums developed as different Jewish groups came to Kabul, there does not seem to have been animosity or even firm divisions between them.[57] No studies have appeared regarding any specific differences between these three quorums in Kabul, aside from the members' city of origin, but perhaps the congregants used distinct prayer melodies. Because of increased emigration in the 1960s, the three quorums eventually converged into two congregations; the Balkh and Bukharian quorums joined together, and the Herati congregation remained separate.[58]

During that same decade, Jewish religious life in Kabul expanded with the building of a new synagogue in a part of the city called Shaar-i-Nau. In 1965, a Lubavitch *shaliah* [emissary of Zion] visited Kabul and criticized the state of Jewish ritual worship there.[59] He was the only known *shaliah* to have reached Afghanistan since 1920.[60] Some Jews already may have considered establishing a new house of worship, but his visit seems to have jumpstarted its construction, which was completed in 1966.[61] The synagogue, named "Shaar-i-Nau" after the area of the city in which it was located, was built on a separate property and included a *mikvah* [ritual bath]. This new synagogue combined *all* previously existing quorums in Kabul, unifying them into one congregation. An interviewee from Kabul vividly remembered the synagogue, as his father was heavily involved in its construction. According to this interviewee, his father supervised the plans for the synagogue's exterior appearance, which included designs composed of six-pointed Jewish stars:

> He wanted to make sure that . . . any Jews that travel around . . . there's a symbol they can recognize and say it's a Jewish place . . . those who don't understand it will think it's . . . Islamic ornamentation.[62]

The very edifice of Kabul's new synagogue served as a microcosm of Jewish-Muslim interaction in Afghanistan. The Jews of Kabul felt sufficiently confident to have visible shapes on the synagogue that were intelligible to Jews, but still not obvious enough to potentially provoke animosity from outsiders. While Afghan Jews and Muslims lived alongside each other relatively peacefully, the Jewish community remained wary of drawing any unwanted attention.

Certain synagogue traditions, in general, were somewhat reminiscent of Afghanistan's patriarchal culture. All of Herat's synagogues and two of the three earlier quorums in Kabul bore the name of the family instrumental in starting them.[63] In Herat, the synagogues were called "Mullah [learned man] Shmuel," "Mullah Yoav," "Mullah Garji," and "Gul."[64] One interviewee from Herat attended the Mullah Shmuel synagogue, which, according to family lore, his own grandfather helped to physically build in the early 20th century. In Kabul, the first three congregations were called "HaGisoff," "Yisrael Cohen," and "Balkhi."[65]

Women in both Herat and Kabul rarely attended regular synagogue services, with the exception of some elderly women who went on the Sabbath. Even when Herat's women did go to a synagogue, they remained in its courtyard "tasting the spirit of the festival service only at a distance."[66]

Some modern ideas, however, may have influenced synagogue norms as well. It is quite telling that the new synagogue built in Kabul in 1966, called "Shaar-i-Nau," deviated from the age-old practice of naming synagogues after the founding family. This synagogue's creation signified a break from certain customs, especially since the multiple prayer quorums in Kabul merged into a single congregation.

All the main synagogues in Herat and Kabul, new and old alike, provided for women's attendance with an *Ezrat Nashim*, or women's section.[67] In Herat's synagogues, the women's section was always on the second floor. Facing the women was a wall lower than the ceiling that contained carved-out geometric figures.[68] One interviewee from Herat said that the women could see the main sanctuary when standing; but not while sitting down. In Kabul, the women prayed in the same room as the men, with a curtain separating the men's and women's sections. Such an arrangement existed in Kabul's three earlier quorums as well as the new synagogue built in 1966.[69]

Though they almost never attended daily services, many women went to synagogue on Jewish holidays and special occasions, such as bar mitzvahs. Women frequented the synagogues especially on Purim, Simhat Torah, Rosh Hashanah, and Yom Kippur. But it was less accepted for single women to go to synagogue in Herat. One interviewee from that city said that "occasionally" young girls came to synagogue, and that his wife attended after she was married. Meanwhile, a woman from Kabul answered in the affirmative when asked whether women of "all ages," and not just the elderly, went to synagogue. It also seems that men and women in Kabul felt more at ease with one another. One couple from Kabul said that men and women could talk to each other in synagogue, though a man would never shake hands with a woman. In Herat, the synagogues' separate floors for men and women created a barrier to social interaction even after services finished.[70]

More progressive influences also began changing certain synagogue practices surrounding the Jewish holidays. Before Yom Kippur, it had once been customary for men over thirteen—past their bar mitzvah age—to lightly strike each other thirty-nine times with a small whip resembling a "leather thong,"[71] whose dimensions were in accordance with the Talmud.[72] They carried out this practice inside the synagogue. The rabbi would hit a man with three sets of thirteen mild strikes each on the left, right, and middle of his back. The thirteen strikes corresponded to a biblical verse with thirteen words relating to repentance, which the rabbi recited audibly. According to an American Jewish woman touring Kabul in 1966, "the younger generation is now breaking away from the observance of this rite—the *Malkot* [strikes]."[73] While Kabul's Jewish community evidently still performed this practice in the 1960s, as she described it then in detail, she simultaneously revealed that this custom had become increasingly unpopular with Jewish youth.

Though Afghanistan clearly remained a firmly patriarchal society, and the synagogue life there did not alter drastically during the 20th century, the Jewish community was nonetheless receptive to outside influences. The Lubavitch *shaliah*'s visit shows that the Jews, particularly in the more modern capital of Kabul, were affected by this newcomer's sway. Also, Kabul's new synagogue Shaar-i-Nau, since it was not named after a single family, demonstrates that the community became open to modifying certain synagogue traditions. Such changes within the Jewish community, however, remained minor and therefore unthreatening.

EDUCATION

Jewish Education

Like many synagogue customs, educational practices in Afghanistan often reflected patriarchal values. Throughout the 20th century, Jewish education revolved around the boys attending *heder*. Literally meaning "room" in Hebrew, *heder* consisted of multiple groups of students studying under one roof. Each group learned various Jewish subjects according to its age level. *Heder*, also known as *midrash* ["study" in Hebrew] or *hamlah* ["room" in Judeo-Persian], took place inside the synagogue, in a single room separate from the main sanctuary.[74] Boys went to *heder* beginning at age three or four, when they started learning the Hebrew alphabet and how to read from a Jewish prayer book.[75] Then they began to study the Pentateuch, starting with Leviticus, and commentaries on the Bible. More learned students, including one interviewee from Herat, progressed to studying the *Shulhan Arukh*, a codified book of Jewish law from the 16th century.[76] Some advanced to studying the Mishna and *Ein Yaakov*, a version of the Babylonian Talmud. *Ein Yaakov* was—and still is—particularly beloved among Afghan Jews.[77] *Ein Yaakov* focuses upon aggadic stories and practical applications of Jewish law, such as instructions for ritual slaughtering and observing the Sabbath.[78] Many boys stopped going to *heder* after their bar mitzvah at age thirteen, when they would join their fathers in business, but several higher-level students went to *heder* until sixteen.[79] In general, independent Jewish learning continued into adulthood;[80] some individuals, including my great-grandfather, created and recorded their own commentaries on the Bible.

Heder exposed the students to multiple languages, especially Judeo-Persian and classical Hebrew. Afghan Jews called Judeo-Persian script "Rashi"[81] (though it bore no resemblance to the printed script often used in published Jewish texts for the commentaries of the medieval exegete Rabbi Shlomo Yitzhaki, nicknamed "Rashi"). Students were taught how to both read and write Judeo-Persian "Rashi" script, while they learned only how to read Hebrew. In addition to the daily prayers, boys learned to read the *haftorah* [sections from Prophets] for their bar mitzvahs; they did not read from the five books of the Pentateuch.[82] The *heder*'s instructor, called a *mullah* [learned man] or *halifa* [teacher], translated a part of Scripture into Judeo-Persian and then asked the student to read that portion in the original Hebrew and explain it in Judeo-Persian.[83] There were also a few Arabic words in the vocabulary of Afghan Jews. One interviewee from Herat said that they learned *tafsir*, the Arabic word for "commentary," when studying the Bible. He explained that *tafsir* referred to Jewish scholars' exegeses. The Jews absorbed this word from the surrounding Muslim society; though Afghan Muslims spoke Persian dialects, *tafsir* was a well-known classical Arabic word. And teachers even used some Aramaic phrases to familiarize students with the language of the Talmud. At the beginning and end of the day in *heder*, the instructor sometimes said, "*Tzafrah tavah*," or "Good morning," and "*Ramshah tavah*," or "Good evening."[84]

Due to their years of formal schooling, Afghan Jewish men were significantly better educated than Afghan Muslims. One researcher, Bentzion Yehoshua Raz, stated that a shockingly high ninety percent of Muslim men and ninety-nine percent of women in the general population were illiterate in Afghanistan by the mid-20th century.[85] These percentages shrank in cities and increased in rural villages.[86] Most public elementary schools provided classes from grades two to six, with a few schools in cities offering classes through eighth grade.[87] Even with these elementary schools, the majority of Afghan Muslim children only attended school for three to four years "because their parents preferred to keep them busy with agricultural work."[88] While only a small percentage of Afghanistan's Muslim population could read and write in their own tongue, the vast majority of Jewish men knew at least three languages: Persian, Judeo-Persian, and Hebrew. Though more fluent in Persian and its dialects, Jews could still communicate in Hebrew and identify Jewish travelers by their use of this language.[89]

But Afghan Jews and Muslims occasionally utilized similar methods of classroom punishment. When a student misbehaved in *heder*, the instructor sometimes hit him on his bare feet using a device called a *falaq* in Persian. Other students removed the boy's shoes and tied his feet to a wooden stick so they could not move. The teacher then struck his feet with another stick until the boy uttered an apology.[90] One Jewish interviewee from Kabul described this process: "They put their feet up in the wooden thing. . . . Have you seen them, in the Muslim society? Wherever Jews go, they are always adopting certain ways of the society they are living with."[91] The *heder*'s instructor used the *falaq* not only to curb classroom antics, but also when he saw students violating the Sabbath, not wearing *tzitzit* [fringes on four-cornered garments], or breaking other religious laws.[92] Though the Jewish population's literacy rate deviated sharply from that of the general Afghan public, the Jews absorbed certain disciplinarian practices from the Muslims.

The Afghan Jewish and Muslim communities also both had a severe dearth of women's education.[93] For most of the 20th century in Afghanistan, Jewish girls did not attend *heder* or receive any formal schooling. They remained at home with their mothers and learned only those practices directly related to maintaining a Jewish home, such as cooking and the laws of ritual purity.[94] They additionally learned how to knit and crochet articles of clothing like head scarves.[95] As one male interviewee from Kabul said, "So the women, they never worked. . . They cooked and they looked after the children. That was the main job they had. And the boys used to go to work with their fathers."[96]

The different educations of Jewish boys and girls reveal how Afghan Jews used classroom instruction and oral transmission as teaching tools. Afghan Jews emphasized formal schooling for the boys, while women passed down to their daughters acquired knowledge about the home and family. But verbal traditions also played an important formative role for men. Several Jewish men knew the Pentateuch by heart, and fathers often taught their sons biblical stories before they went to *heder*.[97] For men and women alike, folklore was a key part of Afghan Jewish life. The folktales preceding the chapters in this book are just a few examples. Afghan Jews transmitted many stories through the generations; tales of "miraculous doings and revival of the dead were told in the mourners' house; stories of salvation and help were told in the days of trouble."[98] Though boys reaped the benefits of formal education, Jewish women were probably as well versed as the men—perhaps even more so—in rich oral traditions.

The Absence of the Alliance Israélite Universelle

A major defining point in the educational life of Afghan Jews was the nearly exclusive emphasis on traditional *heder* during the 20th century. One of the most significant differences between the Jewish communities in Iran and Afghanistan was that the Alliance Israélite Universelle set up schools in Iran, while *none* were established in Afghanistan. In 1898, the first Alliance school opened in Tehran[99] following requests from European Jews concerned about Iran's Jewish population.[100] More schools followed in the Iranian cities of Isfahan (1900), Shiraz (1903), and Yazd (1928), to name a few.[101]

The Alliance provided a dual curriculum of traditional Jewish studies, including Hebrew and the Talmud, with secular subjects, such
as French and mathematics. Other school systems that combined
Jewish and general studies also arose in Iran. The Otzar HaTorah
[treasure of the Pentateuch] schools opened in 1944 and the ORT
vocational schools were founded in 1950. Though most Alliance
pupils were male, the Alliance sought to institute education for
women as well. By 1900, women went to only one of the seven
Alliance schools in Iran. But just several years later, both boys and
girls enrolled in six of the seven schools; in 1913, over 2,000 boys
and more than 700 girls attended Alliance institutions. Even with
the almost three-to-one ratio of male to female students, hundreds
of Iranian Jewish girls received formal education as early as the first
decades of the 20th century. By 1965, over 10,000 male and female
Iranian Jewish pupils were enrolled in the Alliance, Otzar HaTorah,
and ORT schools together.[102]

Meshed is conspicuously absent among the previously mentioned cities where the Alliance opened schools. Persecutions still
threatened the Jews of Meshed through the middle of the 20th
century. In 1946, a riot broke out against the Jewish population
there.[103] It was almost impossible for a Jewish school to open in
Meshed, for Jews could not freely display their religion.

The Alliance network in Iran, aside from Meshed, enjoyed much
popularity overall. It seems that the Alliance's success stemmed
from the Jewish community's *and* the Iranian government's support for improving modern education. The first Alliance school
in Tehran was actually created by local Iranian Jews who had
heard the Alliance had considered starting a school in Iran. Once
the Jews in Tehran opened their school, the Alliance sent them a
director.[104] Tehrani Jews established this school during the reign
of Muzaffar al-din Shah, who welcomed the Alliance's presence.[105]
While elders of the Iranian Jewish community rejected the Alliance
schools, many Jews wanted this infusion of secular education.[106]
Even those who lived in areas without the Alliance network often
attended Muslim public schools during Reza Shah Pahlavi's rule
(1925–1941).[107]

In stark contrast to Iranian Jewry, many Afghan Jews opposed
bringing the Alliance school system into their midst.[108] The extent
to which the Alliance attempted to establish connections in
Afghanistan is unclear, but various sources convey that the Alliance
communicated with Afghan Jews for some length of time. According
to Bentzion Yehoshua Raz, a chronicler of Afghan Jewish history,
the Jews in Afghanistan worried that Alliance schools would draw
their children away from religious observance and "even hurt their
incomes and their central standings in the community."[109] More significantly, one interviewee from Herat said that Afghan Jews repelled
efforts by the Alliance to create a school there in the 1920s/1930s
not for religious reasons, but because they feared that the Afghan
government would accuse the Jews of spying for foreign powers:

> The Alliance, the *shlihim* [emissaries of Zion], they
> wanted to come to Afghanistan. But our community,
> they afraid to allow them to come. For example, Alliance
> come to Iran, brought teachers, and teach them French
> language—English, French. But in Herat, our commu-
> nity did not allow to come. They afraid from the gov-
> ernment . . . Afraid of, for example, the government says
> these people, they are spies. "These people, they com-
> ing, these Jewish people, they are part of the spying,"
> and this and that. You know, because we are Jewish, we
> are under Muslim government.[110]

The interviewee reveals not only his knowledge of the Alliance
network in neighboring Iran, but the Jewish community's dread
of Afghan authorities. The Afghan government was concerned
about its peoples' possible collusion with the Soviet Union,
Afghanistan's northern neighbor and former nemesis in the
Anglo-Afghan Wars. The threats of conspiracy allegations and
government persecutions against Afghan Jews dissuaded them
from seeking or accepting the establishment of Alliance schools in
their community. Whether or not the Alliance actively tried hard
to institute a school in Afghanistan, the absence of the Alliance
network there underscores the severely disparate educations of

Iranian and Afghan Jews, as well as the latter's apprehension about the government's power.

Resistance to Reform

The Afghan government, however, wanted its country's youth—including the Jews—to receive more advanced schooling within Afghanistan's *own* educational system, a move that the Jewish community vehemently opposed numerous times. Jews felt threatened by the government's public schools on several levels. They mainly feared that their children might be physically harmed by Muslim teachers and students. These government schools also taught classes on Islam as a religion.[111] And students were often drafted into the army for "service" to Afghanistan.[112] Afghan Jews thus exhibited intense hostility to the government's efforts to bring Jewish children into public schools and teach them secular subjects. The majority of the community viewed attempts at educational reform as an immediate hazard to Jewish life. As a result, the Jews rejected public education in 1927, when Amanullah (r.1919–1929) tried to institute coeducational schools in Afghanistan. That year, the minister of education visited Herat to take a census of how many Jewish children went to public school in order to encourage families to enroll. The government had built a new school for 200 students and notably expected the Jews to attend. The vast majority of the Jewish community fervently refused to accept the minister's proposal, for this school lay outside the Jewish quarter. Only three families consented to send their children to this new public school. The head rabbis of the community argued with the minister while "Jewish women were demonstrating next to the synagogue . . . wearing black, and black ropes around their necks."[113] The minister of education eventually left Herat, resigned to the idea that the Jews resisted further integration into Muslim schools and society.[114]

Another failed attempt by the Afghan government to launch more secular education for everyone, Jews included, came in 1936 during the reign of Muhammed Zahir Shah. The Muslim authorities again wanted Jewish families to enroll in public schools. But the Jews worried that their children would Islamicize there, or be taken into the Afghan military. The Jewish community even decreed a public fast day to entreat God to stop the "evil decree" proposing that the Jews attend Afghan public schools. The efforts of Afghan officials came to no fruition, and the Jews remained outside the public school system.[115]

The majority of the community also battled fellow Jews who tried to introduce educational reforms. In 1928, a young Jew from Palestine, Naftali Abrahamof, went to Afghanistan in order to teach about Zionism and Modern Hebrew. Unlike the Afghan authorities, Abrahamof realized that Afghan Jews would be slow to accept changes to traditional Jewish education. The government wanted to combine all of its citizens into a single school system, but Abrahamof understood that most Jewish parents were unwilling to send their children to schools farther than the Jewish quarter. He therefore opened his new school in a Herati synagogue with several Jewish pupils from wealthier families. Abrahamof's slogan was, "We are Hebrews; Hebrew we'll speak, Hebrew we'll learn." Using books he brought from Palestine, Abrahamof taught Scripture, Hebrew, English, mathematics, and Zionist songs like "*Hatikvah.*" He also started exercise sessions and introduced breaks between classes. Abrahamof's school somewhat divided the community between those who wanted to send their children to the old *heder* and those who welcomed his new teaching style. The elders especially opposed Abrahamof's school. Some became anxious that the next step would be a communal desire for Jewish children to receive even more secular education and to enter Afghanistan's public schools. Abrahamof fled Afghanistan after the fall of Amanullah's reign in 1929, and his school ceased to function.[116]

Afghan Jews' true resistance to educational changes, whether initiated by Afghan authorities or a fellow Jew, came from a fear of closer ties with the Muslim community. Abrahamof's school met with the most success, but his ideas resonated only with a small number of families. It seems that the Jews opposed his school out of anxiety that their children would enter public schools afterwards, where they would be in danger of vicious attacks, losing their

Jewishness or being conscripted into the army. Abrahamof's stay demonstrates that some Palestinian Jews in the 1920s were aware of and concerned for the Afghan Jewish community, but it appears that no other visitors from Palestine came to Afghanistan after him.[117] Overall, the majority of the Jewish community remained firm in its conviction to continue with traditional Jewish education in *heder*.

We can reasonably assume that the past trauma of the *Allahdad* for Meshedi Jews who moved to Afghanistan heightened the Afghan Jewish community's general concern about mingling with outsiders. Though Afghan Sunni Muslims and Jews mostly coexisted in harmony, the Jews felt threatened by the possibility that their children would closely interact with Muslim youth at school. The Meshedi Jews in Afghanistan were strongly dedicated to and protective of their religious observance. They fled to a different country rather than risk their lives by remaining in Iran to practice Judaism secretly. It is likely that the Meshedis' descendants in Afghanistan, with their communal memories of Jewish persecutions in Meshed, were especially fearful of non-Jews. Since these descendants of the Meshedis constituted much of the 20th century Jewish community in Afghanistan, their outlooks could have easily influenced the views of other Jews there.

Evidence of Modernity

Despite widespread opposition to secular education, certain Afghan Jews felt that learning non-Jewish subjects was a key tool for the future. The children of three families went to Herat's public school in 1927 and more students attended Abrahamof's school in 1928. Though just a tiny minority of Jewish youth went to these schools, their enrollment reveals that some Afghan Jews welcomed newer forms of education.

Even within the traditional Jewish school system, students learned secular subjects. Certain *heder*s in Herat taught basic mathematics,[118] perhaps to aid with business dealings. In rare instances, individual Jewish men even taught their daughters how to read and write.[119] An interviewee from Kabul said that his own mother, originally from the Soviet Union, taught him arithmetic.[120]

Several families, moreover, hired non-Jewish tutors to teach their sons how to read and write Persian. One interviewee from Kabul said that some Jewish children had private instructors. Another man from Herat explained, "My father hired for me a teacher to learn . . . Afghanistan language [*sic*] in Muslim writing, Arabic writing. I learn[ed] with a private teacher with some other boys." The interviewee highlighted that he studied Persian script with a group of Jewish children, meaning that multiple families wanted their sons to learn Persian lettering. The knowledge of reading and writing Persian would help them when traveling across Central Asia. While this interviewee from Herat said that only a few Jewish men knew how to write in Persian, it is significant that certain fathers viewed learning the script as a skill so beneficial that it warranted hiring private teachers.[121]

Even more surprising is this same Herati Jewish man's revelation that his father employed a tutor to teach him English, probably because it served as a major language of commerce in nearby British India. According to this interviewee, the English tutor himself might have been Indian. It is unclear whether he was the same tutor who taught the interviewee Persian script. It is further unknown if the interviewee learned English with other boys, though that was likely the case. Employing an English language tutor was certainly less common than having one for Persian script. Despite its irregularity, the very presence of any English teacher indicates that certain Afghan Jews viewed English as advantageous to one's general knowledge and especially, for economic transactions.[122]

While Jews in *both* Herat and Kabul hired private tutors, only Kabul's Jewish community saw its girls attend *heder*. A married couple who grew up in Kabul during the 1960s—when the husband and his wife went to *heder*—described how boys and girls attended *heder* with the same teacher. Girls and boys sat on opposite sides of the room in separate groups. Their teacher supervised their work and checked the progress of each group. Girls only attended *heder* until age eight or nine, but boys continued until their teenage years. In our interview, the wife recalled that she learned how to write Hebrew in Judeo-Persian "Rashi" script in *heder*. She added that the prayers she knows today were taught to her in school. She and her husband concurred that "not many people sent the girls" and that *heder* emphasized the boys' education. Though the minority of girls went to *heder*, it is still extremely significant that several Jewish families in Kabul opted to give their daughters a formal Jewish education.[123]

Another major difference between the Jewish communities in Kabul and other Afghan cities during the 1960s is that only Kabul's Jewish children—boys *and* girls—went to public elementary schools, where they all received some secular education. Muhammed Zahir Shah's efforts at reform introduced improved education for everyone in the capital city, non-Jews and Jews alike, as these government-run schools in Kabul now required the city's residents to attend.[124] Boys and girls were separated into different schools.[125] No students went to public schools from January until March, when they were closed on account of the winter. During these months, Jewish children went to *heder* full-time, from ten o'clock in the morning to five o'clock at night. In the summer, Kabul's Jewish youth attended public school classes until around one o'clock in the afternoon and then went to *heder*. One Jewish woman who went to public school in Kabul explained that the city's Jewish community had no choice whether to send the children to these public schools, for the Jews had to attend even on the Sabbath. She emphasized that they went to school then because the teacher took attendance, but that Jews refrained from even picking up a writing utensil. She said, "We had to go to school, but we did nothing [on the Sabbath]. We just walked to school, sat in the chair and came back. Just so that they know that we were there. In the morning, they would call our names—who's there, who's not, who's absent."[126]

As the 20th century continued and Afghanistan's leaders attempted to modernize their people, certain Jews, particularly in Kabul, became so receptive to secular education that they welcomed the chance to study in non-Jewish schools overseas. One interviewee from Kabul said that he left Afghanistan in 1965 around the age of eighteen to attend boarding school in England. His parents saw the likely future benefits a Western education could provide, even with the emotional difficulty of sending their son so far away. As emigration from Afghanistan increased in the second half of the 20th century, seeking an education abroad for Jewish teenagers became somewhat more common. Individual families throughout Afghanistan took advantage of opportunities to learn secular subjects through private tutorials and later, through studies in foreign countries.[127]

The Limited Extent of Modernity

Yet a fundamental split remained within the Jewish community regarding education in the public sphere, including the Afghan government's school system, versus education in private Jewish spaces. Most Jewish families, worried that their children would suffer violence from hostile Muslim students who may have never met a Jew before, resolutely avoided enrolling their children in public schools. Afghan public schools thus posed threats of a physical nature as well as a spiritual one, for they taught religion classes on Islam. But private tutorials in Jewish homes, even if the instructors were not Jewish, felt much safer in every respect since they could be supervised by trusted Jewish family and community members. Jewish children in Herat and Kabul received private tutors who taught them Persian lettering and sometimes— even more remarkably—how to read and write in English. Only Kabul's Jewish children, meanwhile, went to public schools during the 1960s when all residents in the city were required to attend. One interviewee from Kabul said, "To elementary school, all the Afghan boys in my time, in the '60s—they went, but before that they didn't go."[128] There is no evidence that Afghan Jews outside Kabul also attended public schools. Herati Jews actively opposed sending their children to non-Jewish institutions. Kabul's Jewish community lost some of this anxiety through the 1960s, as they resided in the nation's capital and were closer to more sweeping educational changes. Still, if the Jews of Kabul during this time had had the choice as to where to educate their children, many probably would have opted to continue teaching them secular subjects solely within the protected environment of their homes and Jewish institutions.[129]

Throughout the 20th century, Afghan Jews retained their communal attitude of caution, even fear, toward their Muslim neighbors and rulers alike. The Afghan regime clearly had a warmer attitude toward the Jewish population, as the Sunni Pashtun government welcomed and encouraged its Jewish citizens to attend public schools. Yet the Jews steadfastly declined numerous times. Even when Jewish children in Kabul eventually went to public schools during the 1960s, parents sent their children because they were obligated, and many were reluctant to do so. In business matters, Jewish merchants did feel comfortable enough to work with Muslims, in part because the very nature of the profession demanded close cooperation with the non-Jewish populace. But the Jews wanted their synagogue life and educational matters to remain solely under Jewish influences, without any government interference. The Jewish community, nervous that the Afghan government would accuse its Jews of espionage and treason, felt that it had to reject the aid of the Alliance Israélite Universelle. In the next chapter we will see that, as the politics of World War II reached as far as Central Asia, Afghan Jews unfortunately found that they had been correct to be wary of outsiders.

The Great Citadel of Herat, 1993.

Photo: © Stéphane Herbert / Globe Vision, 1993. Courtesy of Stéphane Herbert.

Jewish grave in Herat, 2009: After the Aga Khan Trust for Culture's restoration.

The engraving, partially obscured by grass, says: "Here interred and buried is
the modest, pure, and honored woman, Sarah . . . daughter of Yehuda Betzalel . . .
on the 20th of the month . . ."

Photo: Reuters, June 24, 2009.

Ketubbah **[marriage contract] from Herat, 1812.**

World Repository of Ketubbot, the National Library of Israel, 8° 901/424.
Courtesy of the National Library of Israel.

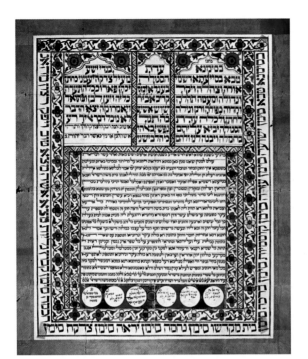

***Ketubbah* [marriage contract] from Herat, 1851.**

World Repository of Ketubbot, the National Library of Israel, 8° 901/425. Courtesy of the National Library of Israel.

***Ketubbah* [marriage contract] from Herat, 1909.**

World Repository of Ketubbot, the National Library of Israel, 8° 901/437. Courtesy of the National Library of Israel.

Model of bride's trousseau chest, Herat, early to mid-20th century.

Collection of The Israel Museum, Jerusalem. Gift of Pasha and Asher Gol; contents lent by Leah Yekutieli, Jerusalem, and Issachar Kort, Tel Aviv. Photo: © The Israel Museum, Jerusalem. Courtesy of The Israel Museum.

Courtyard of a Jewish family in Herat.

Photo: Bernard Dupaigne, 1973. Courtesy of Bernard Dupaigne.

Headstones with Hebrew letters from the medieval period found near the Minaret of Jam, central Afghanistan.

From Kashani, Reuben. Yehudei Paras, Bukhara, Vi-afghanistan [The Jews of Iran, Bukhara, and Afghanistan]. *Jerusalem: Reuben Kashani, 2001.*

Samples of Judeo-Persian letters, called "Rashi" script, used by Afghan Jews.

Afghan Jews used "Rashi" script to write in Judeo-Persian and in Hebrew. This script bears no resemblance to the font used in contemporary published Jewish works for the commentaries of the medieval exegete Rabbi Shlomo Yitzhaki, whose nickname was "Rashi." Above are images of one Afghan Jewish man's unpublished memoir, which he wrote in 1987. First line: "I want to review [events in my life]." Second line: "I was born in Herat in 1906, in the [Hebrew] month of Av."

Photo: © Sara Y. Aharon, 2010.

אם אשכחך ירושלם זאת לי מקדש
תשכח ימיני ושכמי בתוכם

Talmud Torah of Mullah Yehoshua Amram in Herat, circa early 1940s.

My grandfather is the first young man standing on the left. Biblical verses adorn the *heder*'s walls. The *heder*'s dedication plaque, center at the top, says that the schoolroom was built in 1934.

From Kashani, Reuben. Yehudei Paras, Bukhara, Vi-afghanistan [The Jews of Iran, Bukhara, and Afghanistan]. *Jerusalem: Reuben Kashani, 2001.*

Bar Mitzvah in Kabul, circa 1948.

Note the use of traditional Muslim dress as well as modern European clothes.

From Kashani, Reuben. Yehudei Paras, Bukhara, Vi-afghanistan [The Jews of Iran, Bukhara, and Afghanistan]. *Jerusalem: Reuben Kashani, 2001.*

below: The outside wall of Kabul's synagogue and its railings visibly contain numerous six-pointed Jewish stars. They were purposely designed so that Jews would be able to recognize the building as a synagogue, but that Muslims, from a distance, would more likely think the building contained nondescript geometric decorations.

Railing of Kabul's synagogue in 2006.

Photo: Lee Greenberg, 2006. Courtesy of Lee Greenberg.

Kabul's synagogue exterior near the roof, 2011.

Photo: Reuters, June 1, 2011.

The Mullah Yoav Synagogue in Herat, 1993.

Note the garbage and litter strewn across the synagogue's interior.

Photo: © Stéphane Herbert/ GlobeVision, 1993. Courtesy of Stéphane Herbert.

The Mullah Yoav Synagogue in Herat, 2009:
After the Aga Khan Trust for Culture's restoration (1).

Note the synagogue's post-restoration cleanliness. This
synagogue is now used as a school for Herat's (Muslim)
children. The school even contains a television (left-hand
side of the back wall). The restorers know that the building
used to be a synagogue, but the children do not.

Photo: Reuters, June 24, 2009.

The Mullah Yoav Synagogue in Herat, 2009: After the Aga Khan Trust for Culture's restoration (2).

Photo: Reuters, June 24, 2009.

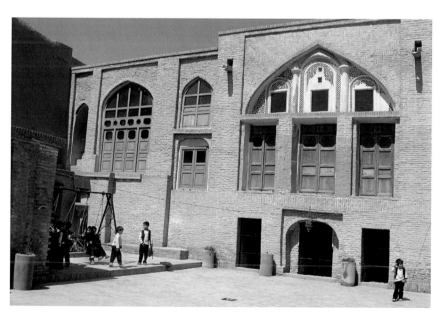

The Mullah Yoav Synagogue in Herat, 2009: After the Aga Khan Trust for Culture's restoration (3).

Photo: Reuters, June 24, 2009.

right: **A 1934 headstone from a Jewish grave lies on the ground inside a mosque's repository near Herat.**

The headstone's inscription is written entirely in Hebrew. The epigraph's top line with the smaller words says, "A Fair Remembrance for a Righteous [Man]." The dedication says, "This [headstone] was built in [the Hebrew month of] Adar in 1934 to sanctify . . . and raise [to Heaven] the soul of . . . Mattatya son of David Diel . . . who passed away with a good name on the fourth of [the Hebrew month of] Av in 1931 . . . at forty-seven years old."

The epigraph then concludes with a biblical verse about eternal remembrance: "And I will give them, in My House and within My walls, a monument and a name, better than sons or daughters; I will give them an everlasting name which shall not perish" (Isaiah 56:5).

This headstone is highly significant as one of the few surviving Afghan Jewish artifacts that contain a specific date. The discovery of the headstone raises many difficult questions; indeed, some of them are almost impossible to answer. When was the headstone separated from the grave—and why? Was the removal of the headstone from the grave for the purposes of destruction or for safekeeping? How and when did the headstone eventually arrive in a mosque near Herat? Is this headstone still laying on the floor of the same mosque today? And would the Afghan government allow this headstone to be moved out of the country to be preserved in a Jewish museum? Even with these queries, the very photograph of this headstone is important as it preserves historical evidence about Jewish life in Afghanistan.

Photos: Reuters, November 5, 2009.

"The Jewish Shepherd"

A king who was out hunting in the desert heard the sound of a flute. Its music was so sweet that he followed it until he came to a hill on which a Jewish shepherd was sitting and piping away. The king took a liking to him and said, "Shepherd, how would you like to leave your flock and come with me?" So the shepherd left his flock and went with the king, who made him the royal treasurer.

But good people create enemies and envy, especially if they happen to be Jews. The king's ministers saw how successful and well-liked the new treasurer was and grew jealous. "We must find a way to discredit him," they said to one another. And so they went to the king and told him, "This Jew of yours is embezzling state funds and pocketing a share of the taxes he collects."

When the king heard this, he grew furious and called for an audit of the Jew's bank account. The auditors went and couldn't find an account in the Jew's name.

"Then we'll search the man's house!" said the king. And so he searched the shepherd's house with his ministers and policemen— but there was nothing to be found there except for some cheap furniture, because the Jews lived as simply as could be.

Only one room even had a lock on it, and it was the last one the king came to. When he asked the Jew's servants what was in it, they answered that they didn't know, because only the Jew was allowed to enter it and he always locked the door behind him. "Do you see now, Your Majesty?" crowed the ministers. "This is where he's been hiding his thefts!" The king ordered the door broken down—but the room, when rushed into, proved to be perfectly empty except for a shepherd's staff, an old knapsack, and a flute.

Everyone was astonished. And when the king asked his treasurer what it all meant, the Jew replied, "Your Majesty, when you made me your treasurer, I put my shepherd's things in this room. Now I come here to play my flute an hour a day in order to remind myself that I was once just a simple shepherd in the desert who shouldn't put on any grand airs." [1]

3

GOOD-BYE,

AFGHANISTAN

—⁓—

"The Jewish Shepherd," a story replete with anti-Jewish sentiment, transmits a strong message of distrust toward the Afghan
government. Pernicious advisors resentful of Jewish wealth sway
the king to suspect his new Jewish treasurer, conveying that Jews
cannot even rely upon their king to support them. The story reveals
the Jews' real-life concern that jealous Afghan rulers might attempt
to frame an innocent Jew and rob him of his status, reputation, and
possessions. That a Jewish man was able to become treasurer should
not be taken as a reflection of the reality for Afghan Jews. Rather,
the story emphasizes to Jewish children the danger of rising to powerful government positions, stressing that it is appropriate to lead a
simple life, as did the folktale's shepherd. The grim story, focusing
on "embezzling" accusations, "thefts," and "auditors," considerably diverges from the light-hearted, fairytale imagery of other
folktales, like "The Princess Who Became a Garland of Flowers"
and "A Treasure from Heaven," which precede Chapters 1 and 2,
respectively. "The Jewish Shepherd" underscores that attempts to
closely mingle with the secular rulers should be avoided, for Jews
would then suffer from life-threatening perils.

If "The Jewish Shepherd," whose date of origin is unknown,
circulated in the 1930s and 1940s, it certainly would mirror the
Afghan Jewish community's fear of the government during that
time. The beginning of Afghan Jewry's emigration marked a sharp
departure from the overall congenial relations that the Jews and
the Sunni Muslims had enjoyed together for centuries. Afghan
Jews and Pashtuns had long bonded over their shared traditions,

including an ancestral claim to the Ten Lost Tribes of Israel. But rising ethnic and religious nationalism in the 20th century emphasized the positions and influence of Afghan Muslims over other groups, mainly in the economic sector.[2] The Afghan regime released a series of prohibitive anti-Jewish decrees, forcing hundreds to flee the country for Palestine and particularly for India.[3] This hostility toward "outsiders" and especially the Jews seems to have been exacerbated by the arrival of hundreds of Nazis in Afghanistan after it signed trade agreements with Germany in the 1930s. The Third Reich, eager to threaten the Allies' stronghold on the Middle East and Central Asia, wanted to infiltrate Afghanistan and gain access to British India.

Despite severe restrictions against the Jews, most remained in Afghanistan because they could not picture their lives improving elsewhere. This mentality changed in 1948 with the creation of the State of Israel. Though some previously had left Afghanistan to escape fierce discrimination, the declaration of Israel's independence was the singular, most powerful force propelling the majority of the community to move en masse. Most Jews felt little compunction about leaving Afghanistan, which suggests that they felt a stronger bond to the newly formed Jewish state than to their country of origin. This chapter, in examining the causes behind Afghan Jewry's emigration, reveals that persecution was *not* the major force driving their departure. This contrasts sharply with the hardships facing Jews in Arab lands, where rapidly growing opposition to Zionism resulted in riots and severe violence. Unlike Afghan Jewry, Jewish communities in some Arab countries ultimately had to renounce their citizenship and assets in order to emigrate. For the Jews in remote Afghanistan, the emotional and religious pull to return to Zion compelled them to leave their native land.

AFGHANISTAN'S PRIORITIES:
NATIONALISM AND NEUTRALITY

After the third Anglo-Afghan War ended in 1919, Afghanistan's independence sparked a fierce nationalism that would thereafter influence the country's domestic and foreign policies. In 1929, a Pashtun banker named Abdul Majid Zabuli, who would become the minister of national economy ten years later, described King Nadir Shah's (r.1929–1933) emphatic belief that "our own nationals" must exercise greater control over the country's trade:

> Today we see in our country export, import, transportation, brokerage and everything else are all done by foreigners; only shopkeeping is left for our people. This situation is intolerable and we must have our own nationals engaged in all these activities throughout the country. We must find a way to cut off the hands of the foreigner.[4]

Upon first glance, it may seem that Nadir simply decried the presence of non-Afghans in his country. But he cited mercantile activities specifically dominated in Afghanistan by local Hindus and Jews (see Chapter 2). His urgent message to Zabuli in harsh, unequivocal terms to "cut off the hands of the foreigner" thus suggests that he did not consider Hindus, Jews, and other non-Muslims as Afghan nationals. More importantly, these "foreigners" posed an economic threat to true Afghans.

Nadir's words here are surprising in light of his new constitution of 1931, which allowed for greater religious expression for non-Muslims in Afghanistan. His constitution became the first to omit *dhimmi* restrictions, which had required non-Muslims to pay additional taxes and wear specific garb. Article 9 of the constitution stated that all Afghans were to be treated equally "without any distinction of creed or religion."[5] Despite the official, legal advancement of non-Muslims in Afghanistan, it seems that Nadir privately sought to secure the position of indigenous Afghan Muslims over other groups.

One means of bolstering the country's (financial) independence was through the creation of a banking system. In 1931, Afghanistan's first joint-stock company, "Shirkat-i-Ashami-i-Afghan," was formed as such in order to avoid Islamic religious prohibitions against banking practices like interest and usury.

Shirkat-i-Ashami was not a vehicle of the state and benefited from both private and public resources. Despite religious concerns, it was dubbed the "Bank-i-Milli," or the "Afghan National Bank," in 1932.[6] Founded by Abdul Majid Zabuli, the Bank-i-Milli became quite powerful, with "a virtual monopoly in the major commodities of the Afghan export-import trade."[7] The Bank-i-Milli's monopoly would prove to be a main cause of the Jewish community's impoverishment.[8]

Nadir also became highly concerned about improving Afghanistan's international relations. He and his successors struggled to assert their country's sovereignty without aggravating Britain and the Soviet Union, the two nations that had fought bitterly over Afghanistan and its routes to India in the Anglo-Afghan Wars.[9] Nadir's foreign policy was guided by a professed dedication to remaining impartial in world affairs, according to the Kabul-based newspaper *Islah* in 1931:

> In my opinion the best and most useful policy that one can imagine for Afghanistan is a policy of neutrality. Afghanistan must always entertain good relations with its neighbors as well as all the friendly powers who are not opposed to the national interests of the country.[10]

During his reign, Nadir aimed to establish harmonious relations between his country and others in an effort to elevate Afghanistan's reputation and status. He confirmed or signed treaties with each of Afghanistan's former enemies, recommitting in 1930 to the 1921 Anglo-Afghan Treaty with Britain,[11] and signing a non-aggression pact with the Soviet Union in 1931. With these agreements came greater economic cooperation, including an increased exchange of goods with the Soviet Union[12] and Afghanistan's acceptance of British aid.[13] Nadir also signed accords with several other European nations, such as Austria, Spain, and Poland.[14] Soon many Europeans from Germany, France, and other countries worked in Afghanistan; the vast majority were not from Britain and the Soviet Union, as too much distrust lingered from the Anglo-Afghan Wars even after treaties were settled.[15]

Nadir's brother, Muhammed Hashim Khan, was the prime minister throughout Nadir's tenure as ruler and similarly remained deeply committed to maintaining Afghanistan's neutrality. After Nadir's assassination in 1933, the accession of his young son, Muhammed Zahir Shah, to the throne paved the way for Hashim and other politically-minded relatives to exert their influence over the newly crowned monarch. Hashim, in particular, continued to exercise much control over foreign policy as prime minister until 1946,[16] and his dedication to Afghanistan's neutrality guided the country relatively unscathed through World War II.

THE NAZI PRESENCE IN AFGHANISTAN
Afghan-German Collaboration

While Nadir and Hashim wanted to strictly maintain Afghanistan's neutrality, they also desperately sought to improve their country's place on the world stage by modernizing its infrastructure and technology. They realized that—even though nationalism demanded independence from foreign powers—the Afghan people did not have the means or the education to modernize their country alone. Afghanistan was loath to involve Britain or the Soviet Union after the Anglo-Afghan Wars, and so it turned to Germany, ally of the Ottoman Empire during World War I. Scores of Germans arrived in Afghanistan during the reform-minded Amanullah's reign (r.1919–1929),[17] and the German presence continued to increase during the subsequent years of Nadir's rule. But it was only under the Hashim-influenced government of Muhammed Zahir Shah that a series of formal accords brought hundreds of Germans from various professions to Afghanistan.

For Germany, a hand in Afghanistan's affairs posed a unique opportunity to threaten both the Soviets to the north of Afghanistan and the British in nearby India. The following excerpt from a telling 1939 memorandum shows that the Third Reich capitalized on the chance to infiltrate Afghanistan. This memorandum was issued by Germany's Foreign Policy Office, also called the "Aussenpolitisches Amt" or APA. It was established in 1933 under

Alfred Rosenberg, one of the major creators and strategists of principal Nazi doctrines. Rosenberg, whose APA primarily aimed to destroy "world Jewry and Bolshevism,"[18] believed that Nazi ideology could be spread through German foreign trade.[19] He wanted to increase the German presence in Central Asia in order to forward Nazi interests, as well as to intimidate Britain and the Soviet Union. This document, written by Arno Schickendanz, the head of Rosenberg's staff at the APA, exposes Germany's intent to create a base in Afghanistan to launch attacks, if necessary, against the Third Reich's enemies.

> In 1936–37 . . . the German Reich and Afghanistan concluded a number of basic treaties covering military, cultural, and economic matters . . . Their purpose was to aid Afghanistan systematically to realize her ambition of becoming more independent of her neighbors. It was the objective of the Aussenpolitisches Amt to make it possible for Afghanistan to remain neutral in the case of a war, or, if the opportunity arose, for the country to be used by Germany for operations against British India or Soviet Russia . . . The German colony developed during that time from an insignificant group to the largest group of Europeans in Afghanistan.[20]

Afghanistan and Germany created a symbiotic relationship in which each felt that it gained the greater benefit. Afghanistan eagerly welcomed German experts in engineering, construction, and technology, whose very presence formed part of "Nazi Germany's concerted drive to penetrate the Middle East politically and culturally, as well as economically."[21] While most of the Germans in Afghanistan were employed in these civilian fields, some also worked with the Afghan military. Germany pledged to send thousands of machine guns and other weapons to Afghanistan, whose army benefited from direct training given by German military officials.[22] Other Germans worked in the communications systems and the Bank-i-Milli, which started a branch in Berlin to ease and encourage Afghan-German transactions. Trade, as a result, increased between the two countries. In 1937, Afghanistan and Germany signed the Todt Agreement, granting Germany the right to manage road construction in Afghanistan.[23] The two countries also agreed in August 1939 that Germany would ship equipment to "textile mills and hydroelectric plants" in Afghanistan in exchange for the delivery of cotton and wool to Germany.[24] The Third Reich's ventures into Afghanistan were evidently more for political and military, rather than economic, gain, since Germany did not make or expect to produce a profit from the trade agreements.[25] As for Afghanistan's expectations, Kabul did not perceive Germany's involvement as colonialist or expansionist, but rather as a means to serve Afghanistan's own needs.[26]

The exact number of Germans in Afghanistan during the 1930s and 1940s is difficult to ascertain. One prominent historian of Afghanistan, Vartan Gregorian, reported that "by 1939, there were somewhere between 100 and 300 German experts and technicians in Afghanistan."[27] The range given above is large and more importantly, it is unknown what percentage of these Germans were Nazi sympathizers or party members. Reuben Kashani, an Afghan Jew who wrote several works on Afghan Jewry, suggested that most of the Germans in Afghanistan were affiliated with the Nazi party. He placed the number of "the German Reich" there at three hundred.[28]

Whatever the precise amount, the considerable number of German officials in Afghanistan enjoyed close personal relationships with Afghans. In 1947, Carl Rekowski, a former consul in the German Foreign Office, signed a war crimes affidavit describing money transfers from the Third Reich foreign minister, Joachim von Ribbentrop, to leaders in Palestine, Iraq, and Afghanistan. This affidavit shows that Ribbentrop made monthly payments to the Grand Mufti of Jerusalem, Hadj Amin al Husseini; the prime minister of Iraq, Raschid Ali al Gaylani, who served in this capacity for several months each in 1940 and 1941; and Ghulham Siddique, the former foreign minister of Afghanistan under Amanullah (r.1919–1929). Ribbentrop sent funds to Siddique, which only became available in 1944, for his "Rent for House,"

"Living Expenses," "Food," and "Personal Expenses."[29] Perhaps Ribbentrop's payments for these individuals' personal needs might seem innocuous, but the classification of this document under the "Office of Chief of Counsel of War Crimes" negates that possibility. These payments, then, may be evidence of a bribe. Even if the money did not come with stated preconditions from Ribbentrop, the funds certainly would be a strong incentive to heed his wishes.

All these recipients, indeed, of Nazi sums were important officials in the Middle East and Central Asia who colluded with Nazi Germany. In 1939, the Third Reich considered assisting an insurrection to reinstate Amanullah through Ghulham Siddique's aid; the Nazis rejected the plan after questioning Siddique's reliability and concluding that such a move would endanger Germany's popularity in Afghanistan.[30] German interference in Afghanistan, as in Iraq and Palestine, played a central part in trying to alter the power balance in the Middle East away from the Allies. The Grand Mufti and Gaylani, highly influential Arab figures in two British mandates, were sympathetic to the Third Reich and also to one another for political and ideological reasons. Both sought to free their homelands from Britain's colonialist regime and felt that a strong partnership with Germany would best lead to independence. Gaylani's coup, supported by the Grand Mufti and plotted in Palestine, deposed the Iraqi government in April 1941 and reinstated Gaylani as prime minister.[31] As Britain's forces advanced toward Iraq in late May, Gaylani (and the Grand Mufti) fled to Germany.[32] In August 1941, Fritz Grobba, the Nazi representative to Gaylani's exiled government and also the former German ambassador to Iraq, recommended that Germany formally recognize Gaylani's government as the true Iraqi leadership.[33]

The Grand Mufti of Jerusalem, too, maintained a close relationship with high-ranking Third Reich officials. When meeting with Hitler and Ribbentrop in November 1941, the Grand Mufti emphasized that "the Arabs were Germany's natural friends because they had the same enemies as had Germany, namely the English, the Jews, and the Communists."[34] Repeatedly using similar language in meetings with Nazi officials,[35] the Grand Mufti

requested a formal declaration of Germany's intent to help lib-
erate Palestine. Though Hitler demurred, saying that Germany
could not overextend its troops, he affirmed that the Third Reich
and the Grand Mufti had common foes:

> Germany stood for uncompromising war against the
> Jews. That naturally included active opposition to the
> Jewish national home in Palestine . . . Germany was at
> the present time engaged in a life or death struggle
> with two citadels of Jewish power: Great Britain and
> Soviet Russia.[36]

By grouping Jews with Britain and the Soviet Union, the two
main foreign enemies of Afghanistan in the modern period, Hitler
revealed part of the lure of penetrating the Middle East and
Central Asia. Nazi involvement there mostly sought to weaken the
Allies' control in these regions, but it also carried the bonus of
harming Jews in the process.[37]

There is conspicuously no mention of Jews, however, in German
foreign policy reports concerning Afghanistan during the 1930s and
1940s. These records primarily focus on Afghanistan's proximity to
India and the Soviet Union. It appears that the small number of
only five to six thousand Jews in Afghanistan did not register enough
with Berlin to make the Afghan Jewish community a target.[38]

The Aryan-Descent Claim

With hundreds of Germans working alongside Afghans in
several industries, it is reasonable to surmise that most of these
Germans shared the prevailing beliefs of their homeland on the
eve of World War II. Indeed, Nazi racial theories seem to have
impacted Afghans' notions of their own heritage, as certain Afghan
nationalists and historians of the 1930s and 1940s started tracing
their origins to the so-called Aryan people. Afghans once took pride
in claiming their descent from the Jews of the Ten Lost Tribes, as
described earlier in this book. Yet Afghan nationalist thinkers and
writers of the 20th century began declaring that Afghans originally
stemmed from the Aryans who, these writers said, first settled

in the northern Afghan city of Balkh and then spread westward into Iran and beyond.[39] Some proponents of this theory, like one magazine author in 1946, wanted to stress that Afghanistan was as significant as other Muslim countries in bringing intellectual advancements to light:

> The country of the Ancient Aryans, or the Islamic country of Khurasan [sic], that is the Afghanistan of today, presented the Islamic world with as many men of science and letters as any single constituent of the Islamic world has.[40]

It appears that the Aryan-descent theory purported that *all* of Afghanistan's Muslims, regardless of their tribe or Sunni/Shiite affiliation, had a common Aryan lineage. Afghan nationalists utilized the Aryan-descent claim to further their goal of unifying Afghanistan's Muslim peoples, who came from different ethnicities and Muslim sects. The earlier professed connection to the Ten Lost Tribes, in contrast, circulated among the Pashtuns, the largest ethnic group in Afghanistan. The Aryan-descent theory thus promoted a much greater nationalistic pride by declaring that Afghan Muslims—and even the main two languages spoken in Afghanistan, Pashto and Persian—shared the same roots.[41]

Though we cannot make a direct causal link between the Germans in Afghanistan and the spread of the Aryan-descent theory, the fact that both arose almost simultaneously during the 1930s signifies that the German presence probably encouraged the proliferation of Afghans' ancestral claim to the Aryans. Enjoying close relationships with the Germans prompted Afghans, desirous of modernizing their country, to avow their common heritage with their technology-driven, successful European "cousins."

While Afghanistan continued to profess its neutral position through World War II, reaffirming its status in 1940,[42] the country maintained firm ties to Germany. Nazi officials reported Hashim Khan's commitment in July 1941 that Afghanistan's troops would come to Germany's aid when needed.[43] It is impossible to ascertain whether Hashim would have actually remained true to his words or reneged on his promise if such a situation arose. Yet his words reveal that Afghanistan, if forced to choose, most likely would have aligned itself with Germany.

But Afghanistan's close relationship with Germany concerned Britain and the Soviet Union. They became increasingly alarmed by the Germans' influence in Afghanistan and their proximity to India and the Soviet Union. In October 1940, the "British and Soviet governments demanded that Afghanistan expel all non-diplomatic personnel from the Axis nations."[44] Germany, in turn, became nervous about Britain's and the Soviet Union's interference; in August 1941, Ribbentrop cautioned "all Reich Germans in Afghanistan that they observe complete restraint for the time being" so that they would not further incite either Britain or the Soviet Union.[45] Though insulted by the order, Afghanistan complied in October 1941, aware that Britain and the Soviet Union had invaded Iran earlier that year when it failed to heed the same command.[46] Bowing to pressure from the Allied powers, Afghanistan eventually demonstrated that its neutrality took precedence over the benefits that a continued partnership with Germany might have brought.

PERSECUTIONS AGAINST THE JEWS
Anti-Jewish Decrees

During the 1930s and 1940s, the rising nationalistic desire in Afghanistan to drive Jews and other non-Muslims from the financial sector was a major cause behind a newfound surge of anti-Jewish edicts. The Nazi presence in Afghanistan heightened this resentment of "outsiders," namely non-Muslims who dominated the economy, and likely perpetuated the spread of the Aryan-descent theory. While the growth of anti-Jewish sentiment in Afghanistan coincided with both the rise in Afghan patriotism and the work of German officials there, Afghan nationalism became the more potent force driving anti-Semitic decrees.

New legal policies issued by the Afghan regime destroyed the Jews' business-based livelihoods and brought many to destitution.

In 1933, the Afghan authorities declared that Jews were prohibited from traveling without specific permits.[47] The government also forbade the exchange of imports and exports without a license,[48] which stripped the Jews of the ability to "carry on an independent trade."[49] In particular, the Bank-i-Milli's monopoly blocked the control "held by the Hindu and to a lesser extent the Jewish merchants on the financial transactions of the kingdom."[50] Between the establishment of the Bank-i-Milli and the restrictions on trade, the Jews were hard-pressed to find sources of income.

The most overt anti-Semitic act was the government expulsion of Jews in September 1933 from certain northern towns, such as Maimana and Mazar-i-Shariff; Jews were permitted to live only in specific cities such as Herat, Kabul, and Balkh.[51] The expulsion further strained the Jews' financial stability. Not only did they need special permits and licenses to conduct trade, but they were forbidden to keep their outposts in towns where they often resided for months and even years at a time for business purposes. In 1950, *The Jewish Chronicle* reported that the travel restrictions caused Afghan Jews' lifestyle to decline so much that families lived in "squalor and poverty."[52]

In addition to the indigenous Afghan Jews, many of the Jews residing in northern Afghan towns were recent Soviet Jewish refugees fleeing from Bolshevism. Afghan authorities, aware that this new influx of Jews came from the Soviet Union, claimed that Jewish mercantile businesses in the north were a mask for Communist involvement.[53] The government evidently grouped all Jews together and did not distinguish between those originally from Afghanistan and the Soviet newcomers. Erich Brauer, who described the Afghan Jewish community in a 1942 article for the journal *Jewish Social Studies*, wrote that the Afghans' supposed fear of Communist spies was a convenient pretext to rob the Jews of their occupations:

> It was alleged at the time that Jewish refugees from Russia were entering the country and that it was therefore desirable to exclude Jews from the area bordering

on the Soviet Union. The true motive, however, was the regime's desire to take over the economic positions of the Jews in those towns.[54]

The plight of the Soviet Jewish refugees eventually reached the ears of Jewish communal organizations overseas—as far away as England. On September 25, 1933, a delegation from the Bukharian Jews' Association in London presented a formal letter to the Board of Deputies of British Jews, imploring for aid for the refugees in northern Afghanistan. The missive describes how the Bukharian Jews' Association received numerous letters from Soviet Jewish refugees in Afghanistan, many of them imprisoned when not expelled to the interior cities.[55] Unlike the small, native Afghan Jewish population, the huge Bukharian Jewish community clearly maintained a much stronger communication network with their brethren scattered in various countries. The Bukharian Jews' Association in London requested permission for the refugees to remain freely in the Afghan northern towns until the rest of their families arrived from the Soviet Union, or to be sent to Palestine. On October 17, 1933, the Bukharian Jews' Association sent a copy of their original letter to the Jewish Agency in London, perhaps because their petition to the Board of Deputies of British Jews had not been successful. A note was added to this copied letter to the Jewish Agency, saying that "the position has become more pressing and 2,000 refugees have arrived at Kabul, who are in need of immediate assistance."[56] The following day, Leo Lauterbach, the secretary of the Jewish Agency office, detailed the refugees' impoverishment in a letter to his superiors:

> Two hundred refugees are reported to be in Mazar-i-Shariff, Ankhoi, and Achja . . . The authorities keep the refugees in prison, and have ordered their removal from the border towns into the interior of the country, so that many of the refugees are separated from their wives and children, who remain near the frontier. The local Jewish community is reported to be both small and helpless . . . The refugees in question

are Boukharian [*sic*] Jews from those parts of Russia and Asia which border on Persia and Afghanistan. Even the wealthy among them have been ruined by the Bolshevist revolution and all, or most, of the refugees are victims of persecution, and destitute.[57]

Lauterbach wrote that 200 Jews were refugees, while the letter he received a day earlier says that there were 2,000. The correct number of Bukharian Jewish refugees in Afghanistan at that time cannot be verified, but it is highly likely that more than 200 Jews fled into Afghanistan and that Lauterbach made a clerical error. He agreed with the Bukharian delegation, saying, "I believe that their request must be dealt with the greatest seriousness and urgency."[58] The plea of the Bukharian Jews' Association seems to have worked, as the Jewish Agency issued several immigration certificates in 1935 and 1936 to Jews in Afghanistan that allowed them to enter Palestine.[59]

For the indigenous Afghan Jews, their predicament only worsened through the early 1940s. Some of their deepest fears were actualized in 1941, when the government obligated all Afghan men, including Jews, over seventeen years old to serve in the army.[60] The draft prohibited Jews from carrying weapons, but required them to perform menial labor such as cleaning animal stalls.[61] The authorities decreed that Jews must pay a war tax, or the *harbiyyeh*, for being "exempted" from the military since they could not bear arms.[62] The Jews received no salary for their work. What little money they had went to their military superiors in exchange for mercy.[63] The government officially nullified the conscription decree in the early 1950s,[64] but it is unclear when authorities actually implemented the cancellation. One interviewee from Herat who left Afghanistan in 1956 said he feared being taken into the Afghan army.[65]

While the relationship between the Jews and the Afghan government clearly deteriorated in the 1930s and 1940s, some Muslims were still willing to continue a cordial rapport with their Jewish neighbors. In one Afghan Jewish man's memoir, examined earlier (see Chapter 2), the author detailed his struggles caused by the expulsion from northern trading towns—as well as his gratitude to a Muslim employer who eventually offered him a job. The following is an excerpt from this memoir:

> After [about] ten years [after getting married in 1924] ... at this time they exiled us from Maimana ... I had a harsh, harsh financial situation. We suffered a lot. In the end, I met a Muslim who accepted me as a paid worker. We traveled to Kandahar, a big city among the cities in Afghanistan ... I was with him for four years. Little by little, I had business ... He helped me very much.[66]

The author not only relates the pain of losing his livelihood, but the financial relief that came after working for several years together with the Muslim who had hired him. In an interview, the author's son confirmed that Jews were forbidden to conduct business "in their own name," but they were permitted to work for Muslims.[67] Though we cannot draw conclusions about the Muslim majority based on an individual case, the memoir does indicate that certain Muslims were open to aiding Jews and viewed their business skills as an asset rather than as a source of competition. Despite the bias against the Jews among Afghan officials, such sentiments did not completely trickle down to the general populace. High-ranking Afghan authorities had the most contact with Germans in Afghanistan and thus, Nazi anti-Semitism likely did not touch the local Muslim population as strongly.

A government order forbidding Jews to emigrate from Afghanistan further exacerbated their troubles.[68] Little is known about this prohibition; its start date as well as the factors that immediately caused the decree have yet to come to light. Most sources simply record the existence of the decree and its eventual end, though these sources disagree as to when Afghan authorities lifted the emigration ban. In November 1949, *The Jewish Chronicle* reported that the government stopped the decree; researcher Nehemiah Robinson recorded that the ban ended in 1950; and the *Encyclopedia Judaica* maintained that authorities lifted the restriction in 1951.[69]

Main Causes Behind Jewish Persecutions

It may be surprising to learn of Afghan-German collaboration before the Second World War; the Third Reich's interest in Central Asia is rarely discussed either by history books or the general media. Upon learning of the Nazis' aims in Afghanistan, one might initially assume that Nazi influence, as in so many other countries Germany infiltrated during World War II, became the principal force behind Afghanistan's persecution of the Jews. However, fervent Afghan nationalism, not the Nazi presence, was the main instigator of anti-Jewish policies in Afghanistan. The majority of Nazis only started arriving there in 1936/1937, when Afghanistan and Germany signed official treaties and large exchanges of goods and personnel commenced.[70] That the expulsion of Jews from Afghanistan's northern cities occurred in 1933, several years before most Germans permeated Afghan society, indicates that the expulsion was not chiefly motivated by Nazism. Afghanistan did not distinguish between its indigenous Jewish population and the new Soviet Jewish refugees in the expulsion, for the regime sought to rid the border's trading towns of any and all Jews. The hundreds of Nazis in Afghanistan ultimately intensified the animosity toward Jews, but this seems to have been an indirect influence on government policies. It was the Afghan regime's internal, insidious jealousy of the Jews and their supposed affluence that primarily led to the expulsion.

No evidence has arisen, moreover, about a concerted Nazi effort to harm the Afghan Jewish population. This should not be seen as a humanitarian gesture. Officials back in Berlin probably did not know of or focus on the Afghan Jewish community, even though Nazis resided in Afghanistan. Key German documents about Afghanistan emphasize India and noticeably do not refer to the Jews, a stark difference from German documents concerning other Muslim lands like Palestine and Iraq. Unlike in Arab countries, where translations of *Mein Kampf* and *The Protocols of the Elders of Zion* circulated, no known anti-Semitic propaganda was published or disseminated in Afghanistan.[71] In individual relationships between Nazis and Afghans, the Nazis could easily encourage any bitterness toward the Jews. But there is no identified documentary evidence that the Third Reich sought to destroy the Jews of Afghanistan. Nor did Afghanistan need Germany as a motivator to promulgate anti-Jewish decrees and force Jews into extreme poverty. After the Germans left Afghanistan in 1941, the trade restrictions remained in effect.

LEAVING AFGHANISTAN
Afghan Jewish Emigration

Despite the temporary ban on Jewish emigration, economic difficulties were severe enough to propel scores of Jews to flee Afghanistan even before the creation of the State of Israel in 1948. About 100 Afghan Jews moved to Palestine, later Israel, between 1935 and 1949.[72] An American Jewish Committee report from 1947 records a higher emigration number, saying that "280 fled to Bombay" from Afghanistan.[73]

Spiritual ties to the Land of Israel also compelled multiple Afghan Jews to leave well before 1948. During the late 19th century, individual Afghan rabbis moved to Palestine to enjoy their remaining years in the Holy Land.[74] And in the early decades of the 20th century, several men, mostly from the devoutly religious city of Herat, traveled to Jerusalem for the Jewish festivals; some of them stayed permanently while others returned to Afghanistan.[75]

The bulk of the community, however, probably would have remained in Afghanistan if a Jewish state had not been established. The State of Israel's creation was the beginning of the end for Jewish life in Afghanistan as many sought a haven. In 1948, a growing exodus of hundreds of Jews continued to flee Afghanistan illegally (because of the government's emigration ban) and travel to India, in particular, en route to Israel.[76] The majority of the community did not perceive any Jewish future in Afghanistan. The Jewish population there plummeted from around 5,000 people in 1948 to 800 in 1968.[77] One interviewee from Herat said that his neighbors left beginning in 1949. He highlighted that the establishment of the Jewish state, in addition to Afghanistan's military draft, compelled him to relocate without hesitation. He explained,

"We did not want to go to the army to mix with non-Jews. Also, because we had Israel; everybody wanted to come [*sic*] to Israel." In response to the question, "Do you think if Israel had not been founded, the Jews would have stayed?," he answered, "Yes. We had no choice. Where to go?" In 1956, the interviewee, his wife, and two-year old son traveled from Herat to Meshed and then to Tehran, where they took an Air France flight to Israel. The interviewee said that El Al "came once in awhile to get the *olim* [Jews moving to Israel], but we came on our own." Certain individuals were so eager to arrive in the Holy Land that they did not need an Israeli flight to get there, but sought their own means of moving. While some left Afghanistan before 1948, only the founding of the State of Israel induced thousands to relocate.[78]

Most of the Afghan Jewish community emigrated in the 1960s. According to *AJYB*, the community shrank significantly to about 1,000 people in 1961.[79] One traveler to Afghanistan in 1966 wrote that there were just thirty-five families in Kabul and thirty families in Herat.[80] Indeed, four of the seven interviewees born in Afghanistan left the country during the 1960s. One woman from Kabul, who was a teenager during that decade, said that most of her peers emigrated before they were eighteen. *AJYB* recorded a steady decline in the Afghan Jewish population, with 800 Jews in 1965, 500 in 1972, and 200 from 1974 to 1979.[81] In the following years, *AJYB* did not report separate Jewish population statistics for Afghanistan.[82] Its Jewish community had essentially vanished,[83] with the exception of the well-documented presence of the single Jew in Afghanistan today.[84]

While Herat once held the biggest Jewish community, the harsher poverty there drove its Jewish residents to emigrate sooner than their brethren in Kabul. Most of the Jews remaining in Afghanistan after 1965 were concentrated in Kabul, since they felt more comfortable in the capital's relatively tolerant and modern culture.[85] The four interviewees who left in the 1960s were all from Kabul, while the other three born in Afghanistan hailed from Herat and emigrated in the 1950s. The construction of Kabul's brand new synagogue in 1966 indicates that certain members of the Jewish community did not plan to leave in the immediate future. During the 1960s, the center of Jewish life shifted to Kabul after the mass emigration from Herat, and because of improved living conditions in Kabul thanks to Muhammed Zahir Shah's more liberal constitution in 1964.

Even though they built a new synagogue, many of Kabul's Jews did not envision that they would permanently reside in Afghanistan. An American Jewish man's anecdote about his travels to Afghanistan in 1971 illustrates the mindset of the Jews there. During his college years, this interviewee went to Afghanistan en route to the Soviet Union and spent time with a Jewish couple in Kabul. He was amazed by the harsh squalor of Afghanistan in general, calling it the most "poverty-stricken" country he had ever seen. He described Muslim children begging in the streets, individuals bringing goats onto buses, and people drawing water from the same stream into which a cow had defecated. Based on his story, the Jews' predicament seemed no worse than that of their Muslim neighbors. On the contrary, the Jews evidently had a more privileged lifestyle due to their emphasis on mercantile trade rather than agricultural development. The interviewee repeatedly commented that the Jewish couple appeared quite jolly; they lit Hanukah candles and ate together with him in their home, which contained electricity. During their meal, the interviewee spoke English with both the husband and his wife. The interviewee also emphasized that this couple had no romanticism about staying in Afghanistan. Rather, it was a question of leaving at the appropriate time so they could maximize their chances of bringing the most possessions with them. They had sent their two sons ahead to live in Israel with a friend, an act that the American teenager could not comprehend at the time. He remembered wondering how incredibly difficult their living situation must have been in order for parents to willingly separate from their children. It seemed to the American interviewee that his acquaintances' relocation from Afghanistan was more about seizing upon the prospect for a better life elsewhere and less about dangers pushing the Jews out of the country. His story reveals that the restrictions abounding in the 1930s and 1940s tapered off in the following decades, at least in Kabul, and that the Jews still in Afghanistan during the 1970s planned to emigrate. Even though some Jews remained in Afghanistan after the 1960s, most stayed only to capitalize on the best opportunity to leave the country.[86]

In Comparison with Arab Lands

On the surface, the hardships Afghan Jews faced might seem to resemble the suffering of Jews in Arab lands during World War II simply because these Jewish populations all lived in Muslim countries. But "Arab" countries, like Iraq and Egypt, and "Persian" countries, like Afghanistan, are so-called and distinguished from one another due to different languages and other significant cultural distinctions. While the vast majority of Arabs and Persians share Islam as a common religion, they have separate historical narratives, complete with differing attitudes toward minority groups. Afghanistan's Jews, while they suffered acutely from government-induced poverty, were less persecuted than Jews in Arab lands. Arab countries, much closer geographically than Afghanistan both to Europe and to Palestine, were thus more directly involved in World War II affairs and particularly with the rising conflict brewing over the Palestine Mandate. Unlike Afghan Jewry, the Jews of Arab regions endured pogroms and continually growing hostility resulting from an influx of Nazi propaganda and especially, from Arab anger toward the newly formed State of Israel.

Throughout the 1930s and World War II, the Jews in Arab lands dealt with considerably more violence and discrimination than their brethren in Afghanistan. Bombs and attacks on shops and synagogues endangered the Jews of Lebanon,[87] Tunisia, Libya, Syria, Egypt, and elsewhere.[88] Iraqi Jews, particularly those in Baghdad, suffered tremendously during one of the most infamous pogroms in an Arab country in modern times. Iraqi Jews called this days-long pogrom the "*Farhud.*" Beginning on June 1, 1941, a total of "179 Jews of both sexes and all ages were killed; 242 were left orphans."[89] The British, who ironically were painted as protectors of the Jews in Iraqi propaganda, simply observed the massacre and did not intervene. This brutality partially stemmed from a preponderance of anti-Semitic propaganda like *Mein Kampf* and *The Protocols of the Elders of Zion*, which enjoyed much popularity in Arab countries. Indeed, an internal Iraqi report about the *Farhud* pointed to Nazi-inspired anti-Semitism as one major cause of the pogrom, saying that "the German Legation had been spreading Nazi propaganda over a long period of time."[90]

Even more dangerous than the Third Reich's influence were the growing tensions in Palestine which, following World War II, significantly exacerbated the perils facing the over one million Jews in Arab lands. Through Israel's establishment and the subsequent Arab-Israeli wars, the riots, murders, and arrests for suspected Zionist activity increased. Thousands of Jews seized the opportunity immediately after 1948 to flee to Israel, but others, particularly the wealthy in Cairo and Baghdad (even with fresh memories of the *Farhud*), chose to remain in their native countries. But eventually, many in the upper classes also decided to depart as they felt continually ostracized and threatened. In 1950, Iraq decreed that Jews were permitted to emigrate so long as they were "forfeiting their nationality," which meant that they were required to surrender their citizenship.[91] In Egypt, under the new regime of Gamal Abdul Nasser, close to 1,000 Jews were arrested in 1956, allowing the government to revoke their citizenship and seize their property. Those who left Egypt were permitted to take only some clothes with them. By the 1960s, the majority of Jews from Arab countries had emigrated, and their numbers continued to dwindle in the following decades.[92]

Unlike Afghan Jewry, the Jews of Arab lands after World War II experienced escalating persecution predominantly caused by the Arab-Israeli wars. They were essentially terrorized with greater severity as time passed. Even in such a precarious situation, some Jews in Arab regions still desired to stay in their homelands and hoped that their circumstances would improve, though this mentality changed as the danger intensified. The worst period for Afghan Jews, in contrast, occurred during the decade after 1933, not the years following World War II. The discriminatory decrees of the 1930s were principally caused by Afghan nationalism, not Nazi-influenced anti-Semitism, and the persecutions against the Jews in Afghanistan declined in later decades. Anti-Zionist fervor barely impacted Afghan Jews. While always wary of their Muslim neighbors, they did not suffer from the mob violence or the constant risk of bodily harm that threatened Jews in Arab countries. Even with a temporary ban on emigration, Afghan Jews were not required to renounce their citizenship or property when the government did permit them to leave. Those who chose to stay had little emotional connection to Afghanistan and planned to depart eventually. Most emigrated because they wanted a better life in Israel, the United States, and elsewhere, and less because of persecution forcing them out of Afghanistan.

Major Reasons for Afghan Jewry's Emigration

Afghanistan's independence in 1919 ignited a surge of nationalism that unified its Muslim populations of various ethnicities, but ultimately hurt the Jews and drove many of them into destitution. Such nationalism called for Afghanistan to modernize its infrastructure without entangling itself in world politics, a complex task given the country's disastrous history with the Anglo-Afghan Wars, and the rising tensions within Europe during the 1930s. Afghans' growing xenophobia also propelled them to wrest control of the economic sector away from the non-Muslim populaces, particularly the Hindus and the Jews. Afghanistan's national bank, the Bank-i-Milli, created a monopoly over the country's imports and exports, effectively shutting out the Jews from trade. They required specific licenses, which they could not readily secure, to conduct business. The expulsion of Jews from Afghanistan's northern towns in 1933 formed the climax of the injurious decrees. The fact that all Jews, whether originally from Afghanistan or the Soviet Union, were ejected from these important trading cities indicates that anti-Jewish sentiment, rather than the professed anxiety over Communist conspiracies, was the main reason for the expulsion. The Nazi presence in Afghanistan likely intensified such antipathy toward the Jews, but Afghan envy of Jewish financial success principally shaped Afghanistan's treatment of its Jewish subjects in the volatile years before and during World War II.

Clearly, the nationalistic desire to rid the economic sector of non-Muslims overrode the previously open attitude toward the Jews prevailing in Afghanistan for centuries. Afghanistan's independence was a welcome phenomenon for the country in modern times, and the patriotic government primarily focused on asserting its newfound political and economic autonomy. In personal interactions within the general populace, some Muslims still hired Jews. Cooperation, then, continued to exist between the two groups on a basic communal level. But the Afghan regime sought to unite its Muslim populations, and pushing the Jews out of lucrative financial positions became one means of doing so.

Even with such hardships, Afghan Jewry was markedly more fortunate than Jews in Arab countries, who suffered from pogroms and mass arrests as anti-Zionist sentiment there mounted. The Jews of Afghanistan, unlike their brethren in Arab lands, were not ordered to surrender their citizenship or possessions when they emigrated. Most Afghan Jews, attracted by the idea of the return to Zion, moved to Israel; the second-largest number headed to the United States. By the mid-1960s, the majority of the Jewish population had left Afghanistan.

The end of the Jewish community in Afghanistan marked the closure of hundreds, perhaps thousands, of years of Jewish settlement there. During the Middle Ages and maybe even biblical times, Jews resided in Afghanistan and found success along the Silk Road. Once they emigrated, Afghan Jews made their way to new lands to start a better life for themselves and their families. The hundreds who arrived on American shores were greeted with both an opportunity and a challenge: the promise of a new life without discrimination also came with the threat of decreased observance of Jewish traditions. The small Afghan Jewish community in the United States, as the following chapter reveals, struggled to keep its own ethnic and religious identities within a sea of other Central Asian and Middle Eastern Jewish populations.

"The Lamp That Passed"

There was a man who coveted his neighbors' silver lamp. One day he went to them, asked to borrow an earthenware mug, and was given it. The next day he returned it with a little mug inside it.

"Why bring us two mugs when you borrowed one?" they asked.

"In the middle of the night," replied the man, "I heard a groan. I went to see what it was and found that your mug had given birth to a baby, so I'm only returning what is yours."

The astonished neighbors said nothing and took the two mugs in silence. The next day, the man asked for a loan of a tin plate. He returned two tin plates and again told his neighbors that the bigger one had given birth. Delighted, they took both.

The next day he came to borrow a glass pitcher, which the neighbors were only too happy to lend him. Nor did he disappoint them, for he brought them back two pitchers, a mother and a child. They were thrilled to have such a good neighbor, who kept bringing them more and more things.

One day the man came, asked to borrow his neighbors' silver lamp, and was given it with alacrity. When several days passed without any sign of him, they knocked on his door and said, "Neighbor, why haven't you returned the silver lamp that we lent you?"

"I'm terribly sorry," said the man, "but what can I do? In the middle of the night, I heard a groan, and when I went to see what it was, I found that your lamp had passed away."

"What?" said the neighbors, dumbfounded. "How can a lamp die?"

"If a cup, a plate, and a pitcher can give birth," replied the man, "what's to keep a lamp from dying?"[1]

4

AMERICAN

BEGINNINGS

—⟋⟍—

The comical folktale "The Lamp That Passed" reveals the central role of trade in Afghan Jewish life. The story stresses the importance of exercising caution in business dealings, even between neighbors. "The Lamp That Passed" opens with a covetous man seeking to swindle a nearby couple. Though the folktale is attributed to Afghan Jewish origin, it is unclear if either the couple or the sly man is Jewish. Since the couple is the innocent party in this story, we can assume that they, at least, are Jews. The greedy man wants his neighbors' silver lamp, and so proceeds to deceive them by presenting double of an item of lesser value than silver, like the earthenware cup and the glass pitcher. After trusting the trickster's absurd claims that the cheaper cup and pitcher multiplied after they "gave birth," the couple ultimately lose their more precious lamp, believing it "died." They never paused to question the man's nonsensical assertions before handing over their costly lamp, expecting that they would soon receive two of it as they had with the other utensils. "The Lamp That Passed" is a didactic tale conveying to Jewish youngsters, who saw their relatives and neighbors engage daily in economic matters in Afghanistan, that they should utilize sound judgment and act with honesty.

Many Afghan Jews continued to work in trade after they moved to the United States, where they integrated elements of their former economic, religious, and cultural lifestyles from Afghanistan into a new way of life in America. This chapter explores the challenges that Afghan Jews experienced in merging their traditional practices and identities with American norms. Most Afghan Jews who arrived in the United States settled in Queens, New York. An integral part of their community is their synagogue in Queens, Congregation Anshei Shalom—the only Afghan synagogue in the *entire* diaspora. Official documents from Anshei Shalom display the introduction of democratic governance into this synagogue, a common practice among houses of worship of all religions in the United States after communities internalize the centrality and role of the U.S. Constitution in American life.

Congregation Anshei Shalom's founding documents, moreover, reveal the obstacles to preserving a specific Afghan Jewish identity in America. In the eyes of the Ashkenazi [Central and Eastern European] American Jewish majority, Afghan Jewry simply blended into the larger non-Ashkenazi population. The longer Afghan Jews resided in the United States, the more they absorbed broader ethnic and religious labels that had been created in Europe, and that American Jews still commonly utilize. Specifically, Afghan Jews came to consider themselves as "Orthodox" in order to clearly separate themselves from other Jewish movements. Categories of religious identification did not exist in Afghanistan, where almost all Jews were strictly observant (see Chapter 2). Similarly, Afghan Jews in the United States started to identify as "Sephardic" to differentiate themselves from Ashkenazi Jews, who comprise the vast majority of the American Jewish community. The "Sephardic" label, a term which literally means "Spanish Jew," is a misnomer for Afghans and other Jews from Central Asia. True Sephardic Jews trace their roots to medieval Spain, while most Central Asian and Middle Eastern Jews believe they descend from the Ten Lost Tribes of Israel exiled from Jerusalem in the 8th century B.C.E. This dwindling of specific identities from immigrants' countries of origin in favor of larger labels, a process called "ethnicization," is widespread across immigrant groups of all backgrounds. But the small population size of Afghan Jews in the United States, especially when compared with other Central Asian communities like Iranian Jewry, more immediately threatens the continuation of a distinct Afghan Jewish identity in America.

Like many newcomers to the United States, Afghan Jews wanted to be welcomed into the fabric of American society; and specifically, they hoped to be accepted within American *Jewish* society. That Afghan Jews had a similar narrative to other immigrant groups makes their story no less important. Indeed, it is the shared, common element of Afghan Jewry's experiences that allows us to apply them to future generations. The acculturation of Afghan Jews to America can thus serve as a case study for the adaptation of other small immigrant communities, Jewish and non-Jewish alike.[2]

STATISTICS ABOUT
AFGHAN JEWS IN THE UNITED STATES

At present, no firm data exists regarding the total size of the Afghan Jewish community in America.[3] Nationwide studies like the National Jewish Population Surveys and localized studies such as the Jewish Community Studies of New York do not distinguish between Jews who come from different countries.[4] But the Hebrew Immigrant Aid Society's (HIAS) archives provide the most reliable information about some Afghan Jews who immigrated to the United States. HIAS alone helped settle 423 Afghan Jews between 1980 and 1991; the organization listed no new Afghan Jewish arrivals to America after 1991.[5] Most of the interviewees born in Afghanistan came to the United States after 1960. The *New York Times* reported in 2001 that 1,000 Afghan Jews lived in New York and 5,000 resided in Israel, the two largest concentrations of Afghan Jews in the world.[6] In 2007, Radio Free Europe/ Radio Liberty declared that 200 Afghan Jewish families lived in Queens, New York.[7] Considering that around 400 Afghan-born Jews came to America by the early 1990s, and perhaps many more arrived outside of HIAS's system, it is likely that over 1,000 Jews of Afghan descent currently reside in the United States.

As in Central Asia, so too in America; the Iranian Jewish population heavily outweighs the number of Afghan Jews. About 35,000 Iranian Jews came to the United States in the 1980s, "of which 20,000 live in Los Angeles and estimates ranging from 8,000 to 15,000 live in New York City and Long Island."[8] Unlike Afghan Jewry, Iranian Jews in America number in the tens of thousands. The disparity in the sizes of these two communities, as we shall see, has significant implications for the preservation of their respective ethnic identities.

THE SOLE AFGHAN SYNAGOGUE IN THE DIASPORA
History of Congregation Anshei Shalom

We do not know when the first Afghan Jews landed on American soil, but the creation in 1978 of an all-Afghan synagogue, Congregation Anshei Shalom, indicates that a large influx of Afghan Jews came to the United States during the 1960s and 1970s. One interviewee, indeed, stated that the majority of Afghan Jews who settled in America arrived in the 1960s. All of the synagogue's founders and original congregants were Afghan Jews. But decades later, conflict arose between Afghans and new Jewish groups, such as Bukharians and Israelis, who had joined the congregation and wanted the synagogue's customs and governance to reflect its multicultural constituency. This divergence of opinion proved to be a microcosm of the synagogue's larger effort to mesh traditional values from Afghanistan with American principles of democracy.

—ɯ—

Anshei Shalom originally began as a *minyan,* or quorum, in 1977 in the home of one Simon Abraham, who came from Kabul. Simon, whose father's name was "Shalom," arranged for the quorum to meet in the basement of his house in Jamaica Estates, Queens. The quorum was quite small at first, but it grew so substantially within a year or so that they moved the prayer services to a bigger house in the same neighborhood. Then in 1978, the quorum bought a separate building in Jamaica Estates and transformed it into an official, full-fledged synagogue named Congregation Anshei Shalom [literally, "people of Shalom"], in tribute to the father of the man who jumpstarted the original Afghan *minyan* in his home. About ten to fifteen Afghan Jewish families founded the synagogue.[9]

During the quorum's stay in the second house, the community hired a cantor who had been born in Bukhara and raised in Afghanistan. Soon after his appointment the cantor visited Israel and obtained his rabbinic ordination during his time there. Upon his return to New York, the cantor, now also a rabbi, served in both capacities at Anshei Shalom. Although the synagogue had not purposely sought a rabbinic leader, the congregation accepted his authority nonetheless.[10]

While Anshei Shalom's congregation originally consisted solely of Afghan Jews, other Central Asian and Middle Eastern Jewish communities also joined the synagogue over the following years. The diverse groups attending Anshei Shalom's services included Bukharians, Iraqis, Russians, Egyptians, and Israelis. Hebrew became the *lingua franca* in the synagogue, mostly because a number of congregants had lived in Israel before coming to the United States. Not only did attendees speak in Hebrew to each other, but the rabbi delivered his sermons and pulpit announcements in Hebrew. The Afghan Jewish leaders of Anshei Shalom, who greeted the newcomers with open arms, were pleased to expand their congregation and their membership base. The synagogue utilized a *nusah*, or prayer version, called *Edot Ha-mizrah*, the main *nusah* used in Afghanistan as well as much of the Middle East, including Israel. The *Edot Ha-mizrah* version was thus familiar to many attendees from their countries of origin. The significance of utilizing this *nusah* in both Afghanistan and the United States is further discussed later in this chapter.[11]

With so many congregants of different backgrounds, tensions between some members over the synagogue's leadership eventually heightened to the extent that two groups broke away from the synagogue to start their own congregations. In 2007, the board of Anshei Shalom was not successful in finalizing the rabbi's contract for reasons that interviewees would not reveal. This rabbi was the first one the congregation ever hired, the same cantor who had returned with his ordination from Israel in hand, and had remained the synagogue's sole rabbi for over twenty-five years. The rabbi left the synagogue and formed his own congregation, taking a large number of Anshei Shalom members with him. Mostly Bukharians followed the rabbi since he literally spoke their language. Another split from Anshei Shalom came later that same year, perhaps in part because a taboo against leaving the synagogue already had been broken. This second group, comprising native Israelis in Anshei Shalom, felt unrepresented among the synagogue's Afghan leadership and also formed a separate congregation. Although Anshei Shalom's board continually emphasized that the synagogue, including its board positions, remained open to any and all attendees, the synagogue's highest position of president had always been filled by Afghan Jews and had been unofficially reserved for that constituency since Afghan Jews founded Anshei Shalom.[12]

In both break-away instances, almost all Afghan members remained with Anshei Shalom because they felt greater loyalty to their synagogue than to either of the groups that left. Afghan Jews originally constituted one hundred percent of both Anshei Shalom's membership and its participants. Right before the two break-aways in 2007, Afghans still comprised the majority of the synagogue's membership, but only about twenty-five percent of the individuals who went to services. After the quorums separated, the congregation shrank significantly in size and Afghan Jews, still the majority of the official membership, comprised around forty percent of the attendees. On a practical level, this meant that more Afghan Jews paid synagogue dues than any other group, but one walking into Anshei Shalom would find a sanctuary filled mostly with non-Afghan participants.[13]

The history of Anshei Shalom illustrates that the patriarchal nature of the community in Afghanistan was somewhat carried over to the synagogue in America. The very name of the synagogue, "Anshei Shalom," followed the Afghan Jewish norm of dedicating a synagogue to the family who founded it, like the Mullah Shmuel or Mullah Yoav synagogues in Herat. It is possible that "Anshei Shalom," which can alternatively mean "people of peace," purposely carries a double significance. But all interviewees familiar with Anshei Shalom's history said that the synagogue was named after Simon Abraham's father alone; none suggested that deeper connotations lay beneath the synagogue's name.[14] Even within Queens, an Iraqi Jewish quorum called Congregation Bene Naharayim [Children of the Rivers] testifies to its members' strong traditional connection to the Tigris and Euphrates Rivers of their native land. While the congregants of these Afghan and Iraqi synagogues hail from Muslim countries, the name "Anshei Shalom" displays gratitude and respect to an individual rather than to a shared place of origin.

The functioning of Anshei Shalom's board, furthermore, was strikingly similar to the manner of the *hevra* in Afghanistan, an internal Jewish body that supervised the private affairs of the community. Just as the *hevra* was composed of the most important Jewish families, Anshei Shalom's highest-level board position was unofficially reserved for Afghan Jews, who held the strongest influence in synagogue affairs.

The successive occurrences of the two break-away quorums also convey that personal honor, a distinctive feature of tribal societies, factored into decision-making within the synagogue. The quorums left Anshei Shalom because they wanted greater respect, rather than any changes to religious practices. The Israelis' claim that Anshei Shalom's board should equally reflect its constituency conflicted with the Afghans' desire to preserve the character and leadership of the synagogue they had founded.

As of 2011, Anshei Shalom remained a separate congregation from the two break-away quorums, but nonetheless the three have maintained normalized relations with one another, and all appeared content with their respective decisions. Anshei Shalom took strides to put the previous controversies behind it and focused on rebuilding the synagogue, literally and figuratively. The synagogue planned for constructing a new wing, showing that Anshei Shalom prepared for an increased number of participants despite the break-away incidents. Anshei Shalom also hired a new rabbi of Bukharian parentage who had been born and trained in Israel. The synagogue traditionally welcomed rabbinic leaders of non-Afghan descent; as mentioned, the former rabbi was born in Bukhara (though raised in Afghanistan). Tensions with the original rabbi, then, evidently resulted more from personality clashes than from ethnic or religious divisions. The concerns over maintaining Afghan leadership of the board, which made and implemented any and all decisions regarding the synagogue, did not extend to hiring a rabbi. In interviews, Anshei Shalom's leaders particularly emphasized that they actively sought to engage the younger generation. The new rabbi, unlike his predecessor, was required to deliver speeches in English instead of his native Hebrew so that the synagogue's American-born congregants could readily understand him. Anshei Shalom's board members also expressed their hope that both new-comers and former congregants would feel welcome and comfort-able attending the synagogue, and that relations between Anshei Shalom and the two quorums would continue to improve.[15]

Democracy and the Synagogue

Congregation Anshei Shalom, over the years, increasingly incorporated American democratic principles and the "rule of law" alongside patriarchal values into the synagogue's gover-nance. I examined three central documents from Anshei Shalom: its Certificate of Incorporation from 1978; its first set of bylaws from 1980; and a second, revised set of bylaws from 2002. The synagogue's organizational system itself was modeled after the structure of the U.S. Constitution. The first bylaws consisted of twenty-three numbered items along with several subsections. These bylaws explicitly mentioned the positions of president and vice-president, as well as the appropriate processes for gathering dues and adding bylaws and amendments. As in the American gov-ernment, the president of this synagogue held the most influence of any single position, but his power was checked by a legislative body. Anshei Shalom's president, for example, could only suspend or abrogate bylaws together with the board of directors. The revised set of bylaws from 2002 was over twice as long as the original and followed standard American legal style with articles and adden-dums. These later bylaws described in greater detail the functions of the executive board, the trustees, the rabbi, and membership fees. Requiring a governing board, dues, etc. deviated completely from synagogue practices in Afghanistan, where voluntary donations supported the synagogues' upkeep.[16]

Anshei Shalom's founders, with the guidance of professional legal counsel, were careful to integrate existing state laws into the synagogue's governance as well. Anshei Shalom's Certificate of Incorporation cited and closely followed the language of New York State's Religious Corporations Law, Sections 191 and 193, which detail the formal procedure for starting a house of worship. Both the Certificate of Incorporation and New York's Religious Corporations Law discussed the requirement for a presiding officer and two members at the proceedings, indicating that the Afghan Jews who signed the Certificate of Incorporation were familiar with the text of the Religious Corporations Law and recognized the necessity of heeding its prescriptions. Anshei Shalom's Certificate of Incorporation also underscored the need for annual elections for trustees. The members' immediate call for elections upon founding the congregation reveals that they wanted to mirror the composition of American law. Their synagogue provided for many Afghan Jews' initial encounters with participatory democracy in a Jewish institution.[17]

The leaders of Anshei Shalom also democratized certain aspects of ordinary Jewish life in Afghanistan. The first set of bylaws from 1980 said that "any and all forms of commercialism during the services in the synagogue shall be prohibited." Forbidding business dealings harkens back to the strong mercantile trade in which most Jews in Afghanistan partook, and demonstrates the board's concern that attendees would discuss economic issues during prayer. Yet the second bylaws of 2002 did not include the previous prohibition on commercialism, which potentially reveals that a synagogue norm—of not talking about or conducting business transactions during prayer—had developed over the two decades between the sets of bylaws. According to researcher Erich Brauer, the *hevra* in Afghanistan employed "fines and corporal punishments" for those who violated the sanctity of the synagogue, but synagogue leaders in America, including those of Anshei Shalom, obviously never utilized physical punishment and turned only to monetary penalties.[18]

As was common among American synagogue regulations, Anshei Shalom's members who failed to pay their dues within a certain period of time were suspended from membership rights, such as holding "elective office." [19] The fact that Anshei Shalom's founders chose to include only financial penalties for errant members highlights the discontinuities from Afghan custom. [20]

Also, the growing focus on women's participation in Anshei Shalom reveals that its leaders internalized this general American value as well as certain American synagogue norms. The original Afghan Jewish quorum in New York—like all those in Afghanistan—contained a women's section, which just a few elderly women frequented. [21] Though women went to services from the *minyan*'s inception, neither the 1978 Certificate of Incorporation nor the 1980 bylaws mentioned women. But the 2002 revised bylaws called for Anshei Shalom's Sisterhood Committee, started years earlier, to contribute more actively to the synagogue. The articles relating to the Sisterhood, on the one hand, reflected traditional gender roles, as the bylaws stated that the Sisterhood was responsible for food maintenance like "organizing *kiddushim* [food services after prayer] and *seuda shlishit* [the third Sabbath meal]." On the other hand, the bylaws supported creating more opportunities for women's learning, saying that the Sisterhood should "sponsor activities and *shiurim* [classes about Judaism] for the women of the synagogue." Anshei Shalom over the years increasingly adopted governing structures of the United States *and* called for women's greater involvement in synagogue life. [22]

Such democratization of religious institutions often takes place among Jewish *and* non-Jewish communities in the United States. Houses of worship—for peoples of many faiths—tend to be governed by constitutions, some with multiple sets of amendments, which echo the American system of government. [23] In just one example, a certain mosque in Brooklyn, unlike those in Muslim countries, has an official membership and an elected board to oversee the mosque's affairs. [24] Anshei Shalom followed a common pattern of countless immigrant groups in the United States who similarly shaped their religious institutions after their new country's governance. Modeling houses of worship along democratic lines reflects a community's understanding of American law and can aid its acculturation into American society.

The modernity entering Afghanistan during the second half of the 20th century somewhat familiarized Afghan Jews with certain democratic and secular ideals that they later accepted more fully in the United States. Particularly after Afghanistan's new constitution in 1964, the concepts of representative government touched the Jewish population of Kabul. While such notions were uncommon in Herat and not widespread even in Kabul, the mercantile nature of the Jewish community promoted constant travel between Afghan and foreign cities, where Jewish men became exposed to progressive ideas. Upon settling in New York, the heads of the Afghan Jewish quorum were eager to be formally recognized as a synagogue by New York State, and to model the American legal process in their own congregation by creating a constitution complete with bylaws and amendments. They could have remained as a quorum in someone's home, but they chose instead to purchase the synagogue property in 1978 and file for a Certificate of Incorporation soon afterwards. Contact with Westernization during journeys across Afghanistan and other lands seems to have help eased Afghan Jews' later move to New York and their integration of democratic governance into their synagogue.

EDUCATION

As with synagogue life, so too with Jewish education; Afghan Jews sought to mesh their traditions with modernity. When they came to America, many did not practice Judaism as strictly as in their country of origin. Some would handle money and drive on the Sabbath, acts which would have infuriated the *hevra* in Afghanistan. At first, Afghan Jews in the United States also were unconcerned about engaging in formal Jewish studies. Most originally enrolled their children in public schools—perhaps, in part, because they simply had never heard about their local Jewish day schools. But even parents familiar with these schools usually felt that their tuitions were too expensive. Over time, Afghan Jews registered their children not only for after-school Jewish programs, but specifically for full-time yeshivas with predominantly Ashkenazi student bodies. Many of the interviewees born in Afghanistan initially sent their children to American public schools, yet they increasingly wanted to provide formal Jewish education for their children.[25]

It may seem surprising that a community which once adhered so strictly to traditional Judaism experienced a large drop in Jewish observance after coming to the United States. Upon closer inspection, however, we find that certain aspects of life in Afghanistan influenced this subsequent decline in religious observance, as well as many Afghan Jews' openness to sending their children to American public schools. One woman who went to *heder* in Kabul claimed that the lower levels of observance stemmed from inadequate religious education Jewish children received in Afghanistan. She explained:

> The problem was in Afghanistan, we kept everything without knowing...We kept *Shabbos* [the Sabbath] without knowing. If I went to my parents and asked why we were keeping *Shabbos*, they couldn't answer us ...Whatever we did, we didn't know. That's it. When we kept *kashrut* [kosher], we don't know; when we kept *Pesach* [Passover] . . . Because even the oldest, like the parents were not well-educated to teach the kids. That's what the problem was. That's why when they came here, they became too Americanized and they forgot everything.[26]

Though the level of actual observance in Afghanistan remained high, Jewish education there focused more on the details of practical rituals surrounding the home than on the underlying foundations of the traditions. According to this interviewee, formal Jewish schooling in Afghanistan did not provide sufficient motivation to practice Judaism at the same level in the United States as in their native country. Also, no Afghan Jewish *hevra* existed in America to punish religious infractions.

The almost complete absence of intermarriage in Afghanistan, moreover, played a particularly important role in many Afghan Jewish parents' original decision to send their children to American public schools, even for those aware of Jewish day schools.[27] Unexposed to the "threat" of marrying non-Jews in Afghanistan, most Afghan Jews viewed Jewish education in the United States as a costly ideal. Practically speaking, they did not feel that sending children to public schools "sacrificed" Jewish values. Many Afghan Jews registered their children in public schools simply because they were free. Several other Afghan Jewish families, meanwhile, opposed the notion of their children interacting with non-Jews in American schools, an outlook which reflects the mentality held by most of the Jewish community while in Afghanistan.[28] But the majority of Afghan Jews in the United States were unconcerned about marrying out of the Jewish faith because of the nearly one hundred percent Jewish in-marriage rate in Afghanistan.

The required attendance of Jewish children in Kabul's public schools during the 1960s also may have contributed to the relative comfort some Afghan Jews felt in sending their children to public schools in America. Kabul had obligated all of the city's children to go to these government-run schools, and so a number of Afghan Jewish families were already familiarized with sending their children to non-Jewish institutions.

Despite the original decline in religious observance in America, certain Afghan Jews—mainly those involved with Anshei Shalom— wanted to retain certain aspects of Afghanistan's Jewish educational life. Anshei Shalom's Certificate of Religious Incorporation from 1978 stated that one purpose of the synagogue was "to establish and maintain a school for Hebrew and religious education," a statement absent in both sets of bylaws.[29] Conducting classes within the synagogue was the Jewish norm in Afghanistan, where *heder*s took place inside the houses of worship.[30] That Anshei Shalom never established its own Jewish school, coupled with the fact that the bylaws did not address this idea, conveys that members who wanted to send their children to Jewish day schools were probably doing so already.

After decades in the United States, most Afghan Jewish parents enrolled their children in Jewish schools because, as one interviewee said, they wanted to "return to their roots" as they aged.[31] A large number of interviewees expressed their belief in the critical role of Jewish education in establishing a religious groundwork in their children's lives. Unlike *heder* in Afghanistan, children in American Jewish educational institutions often spend much more of their time and formative years in school than at home. Many interviewees also concurred that some children of Afghan Jewish descent became more observant than their parents because these children attended full-time Jewish schools in the United States. One interviewee remarked, "Yeshivas keep the frame[work]."[32] Though many Afghan Jews did not worry about maintaining Jewish traditions when they first arrived in America, they later felt that the increased threat of assimilation made turning to Jewish education a necessity rather than an ideal.[33]

Like the democratization of synagogues, these trends in Jewish education are not unique to the Afghan Jewish community. One researcher on Iranian Jewry in Los Angeles wrote that Iranian Jewish arrivals in the United States sent their children to public schools because they did not realize "the importance of sending them to Jewish schools;"[34] this stated "importance" seems to refer to the schools' roles in preventing assimilation. The Iranian Jewish community developed increasing concerns about intermarriage in the United States and its threat to the family unit, which led to growing enrollments in Jewish day schools.[35] Iranian Jews reluctant to send their families to Jewish schools were nervous about a potential split in religious practices between themselves and their children.[36] Afghan Jewry's emphasis on utilizing educational resources to promote traditional observance commonly occurs among other Jews from Central Asia and probably elsewhere as well.

While most children of Afghan Jews at present have attended Jewish day schools, some families feel ambivalent about their children receiving a religious education for several reasons. The tuition costs of these schools, as for many Jews in the United States from all backgrounds, remain a significant deterrent. Some parents also fear that their children would attempt to change household norms and create a more observant atmosphere that would make the parents uneasy. One woman from Herat, who strongly believed that Jewish children should attend yeshivas, said that several of her Afghan Jewish acquaintances in America felt differently and worried that their children would pressure them not to watch television or use electricity on the Sabbath.[37]

Yet the majority of Afghan Jews today send their children to Jewish day schools, a trend revealing that Jewish educational institutions in America, in general, are fulfilling certain purposes synagogues once served in Afghanistan. In their country of origin, Afghan Jews' synagogues and the Jewish home were the hubs of religious activity. Jewish schools in the United States, meanwhile, more powerfully inspire observance than synagogues. Anshei Shalom, as with most synagogues in America, is the location for manifesting, rather than implanting, Jewish practices. One interviewee from Kabul agreed that more Afghan Jews observe Jewish customs today, "Not because of the synagogue, but because they go to yeshivas . . . Synagogue is a place of prayer. It's not a school."[38] While the synagogue in Afghanistan remained the center of Jewish life and education was secondary, the reverse occurred in the United States. In the consciousnesses of many Afghan Jews, Jewish education became more primary than the synagogue in shaping children's religious observance.

IDENTITY SHIFTS
Changes to Religious Identity

In addition to the concern about preserving traditional practices, Afghan Jews were hard-pressed to retain their religious and ethnic identities. The longer they lived in the United States, the more they defined themselves along Ashkenazi constructs of different types of Judaism.[39]

Afghan Jews, for instance, began considering themselves specifically as "observant" and eventually, as "Orthodox" Jews. Anshei

Shalom's Certificate of Religious Incorporation from 1978 generically stated that one purpose of the synagogue was "to establish and maintain a synagogue for religious worship and prayer in accordance with the customs of the Jewish religion." There was no mention of Afghanistan or any details regarding what the "Jewish religion" might entail. The concept of a single, unified manifestation of Judaism almost certainly stems from the fact that nearly all Jews in Afghanistan observed the same religious practices.[40] But Anshei Shalom's first set of bylaws from 1980 demonstrates that Afghan Jews in America felt the need to distinguish themselves from other Jewish groups and detail the synagogue's *halakhic* standard. These bylaws qualified the Certificate of Incorporation by saying, "It is the intention of this Organization to attend of [*sic*] the needs of the Afghan Jewish community." Just two years after drafting the Certificate of Religious Incorporation, Anshei Shalom described itself as a congregation officially founded for Jews from Afghanistan. The bylaws here likely reflect a growing presence of non-Afghan attendees in the synagogue, and the Afghan Jewish leaders' desire to maintain the Afghan identity of Anshei Shalom.[41]

Another specific goal of the congregation, according to its first set of bylaws, was "to establish a synagogue in accordance with the traditional laws and principles as prescribed in the Shulhan Arukh" in order to "promote and advance the culture and practice of the traditional Jewish faith among the Jewish community." The Shulhan Arukh, written by Joseph Caro in the 16th century, is a codified work of Jewish law.[42] The bylaws were probably responding to Afghan Jews' decreased observance during the first couple of decades they lived in America. This document emphasized that the synagogue sought to enhance religious Judaism. Even if amendments would be needed in the future, the bylaws stressed that "the form of worship in the synagogue shall never be changed to conflict with the Shulhan Arukh." They also explicitly stated that "the membership, with the approval of the Board of Trustees, may engage the services of a Rabbi who shall be a graduate of a recognized Yeshiva, and also be acceptable as a member in an Orthodox Rabbinical organization." Though the congregation did not describe itself as Orthodox here, it preferred a religious leader with an Orthodox background. In a sharp demarcation from norms in Afghanistan, where the position of *mullah* was passed down in families, Anshei Shalom officially wanted a seminary-trained rabbi. After several years in the United States, Afghan Jews felt that an Orthodox rabbi specifically would best encourage adherence to the Shulhan Arukh.[43]

Congregation Anshei Shalom as a whole ultimately identified as an Orthodox synagogue, as the revised set of bylaws from 2002 illustrates. These bylaws stated that a purpose of Anshei Shalom was "to advance the cause of Orthodox Judaism and preserve the customs and traditions of the Afghan, Orthodox Jewish community." Unlike the 1980 bylaws, those from 2002 combined the idea of an Orthodox congregation with the Afghan character of the synagogue. Anshei Shalom distinguished itself as a uniquely Afghan Jewish congregation that also followed Orthodox customs. The revised bylaws continued that the synagogue supported "the establishment of Orthodox Jewish religious schools." They further stated that the synagogue followed "Orthodox Jewish Halacha [*sic*] . . . as prescribed in the Shulhan Arukh." This was the first time where the synagogue's practices were specified as Orthodox (and not just in accordance with the Shulhan Arukh). The document additionally emphasized piety by saying that "members of the synagogue are expected to attend its prayer services . . . and make the Halacha [*sic*] a significant influence in their daily lives." The requirements for the rabbi, too, were more detailed in the revised bylaws than in previous texts. An incoming head rabbi could not simply obtain his ordination from an Orthodox yeshiva, but he also must have served in an Orthodox synagogue for at least one year. Any new cantor at Anshei Shalom similarly had to have previously worked in an "Orthodox Jewish synagogue" for a minimum of one year.[44]

It was clearly important to the synagogue's leadership to hire Orthodox religious figures—but Afghan Jews *also* came to consider themselves as Orthodox and believed that Orthodoxy resembled their traditional religious observance in Afghanistan. That many congregants internalized Ashkenazi patterns of Jewish identity became evident in the interviewees' manners of speech. Almost all interviewees, whether they grew up in Afghanistan or not, used common Yiddish words and pronunciations such as *daven* [pray], *shul* [synagogue], and *Shabbos* [the Sabbath]. One man from Kabul described the first Afghan Jewish quorum, saying, "We were not a very Orthodox *shul*. People would come with a car. But the service, everything, was Orthodox."[45] In addition to utilizing Ashkenazi terminology, the interviewee revealed his outlook that driving on the Sabbath was a practice that distinguished between different types of Judaism.[46] For the interviewee, arriving in a car at synagogue was not accepted in Orthodoxy and conflicted with the Judaism to which he subscribed. The participants demonstrated that Afghan Jews, and not just the synagogue's founders, commonly absorbed Ashkenazi norms of Jewish identity.

The descriptions in Anshei Shalom's legal documents about adhering to a certain wing of Judaism and to the Shulhan Arukh follow a widespread approach that many synagogues in New York and elsewhere have taken. As early as 1931, the Certificate of Incorporation of Manhattan's Jewish Center stated that "the observances and the religious form of the worship and celebration . . . shall be in accordance with the Jewish orthodox [*sic*] faith, and . . . the rules and precepts of orthodoxy as contained in the Shulchan Aruch [*sic*] . . . shall be conclusive and binding." The 1948 synagogue constitution of the Leo Baeck Temple in Los Angeles said the congregation followed Reform Judaism; the 1968 constitution of the Northern Hills Synagogue, Congregation B'nai Avraham in Cincinnati emphasized Conservative Judaism. The 1972 Certificate of Incorporation and bylaws from Congregation Kehillath Jeshurun in New York declared that "the purpose of the Congregation is to maintain and conduct an Orthodox synagogue in conformance with the dictates of the Written and Oral Law, as articulated in the Shulhan Aruch [*sic*] and its commentaries." The leaders of Anshei Shalom, in characterizing their own synagogue as "Orthodox," emulated standard formulations found in the documents of synagogues across the United States.[47]

Changes to Ethnic Identity

In addition to absorbing the idea of sectarian Judaism, the Afghan Jewish community came to identify with American Jewry's often-used label for non-European Jews—"Sephardic." The term "Sephardic" originally referred exclusively to the Jews expelled from Spain in 1492 and their descendants; "Sepharad" is the Hebrew word for "Spain." Over time, "Sephardic" became a colloquial reference for Jews not just from the Iberian Peninsula, but also from North Africa, the Middle East, Central Asia, and the Balkans. Essentially, "Sephardic" today is used to denote "almost any Jew who is not Ashkenazi."[48]

Of the three documents I examined from Anshei Shalom, only the most recently revised bylaws from 2002 contained the word "Sephardic," specifically when referring to the synagogue's choice of prayers:

> Prayer services shall be the Orthodox Jewish Sephardic prayer service as practiced by the Afghan Orthodox Jewish communities (with an emphasis on preserving their unique traditional prayers and characters).[49]

While the term "Orthodox" was included in both the 1980 and 2002 bylaws, "Sephardic" first appeared more than two decades after the founding of the synagogue. Perhaps the concept of Orthodoxy was easier for Afghan Jews to incorporate into their consciousnesses because it qualified already existing observance levels, whereas the Sephardic identification might have jeopardized the Afghan character of the congregation. Indeed, the 2002 bylaws were explicitly concerned with maintaining distinct Afghan Jewish customs.[50]

The interviewees' usage of "Sephardic" further conveys that much of Afghan Jewry as a whole came to consider itself "Sephardic" alongside its Afghan identity. One interviewee from Kabul remarked that he identified fully as an Afghan Jew before arriving in America, where he started to view himself as "Sephardic."[51] One young interviewee born in the United States said that she identified as both an Afghan Jew and a Sephardic Jew because she had family from

Afghanistan as well as the Middle East.[52] A married couple from
Kabul also called themselves "Sephardic" and "Afghan," though
they asserted that they had been born and raised in Afghanistan.[53]
The husband then depicted what he termed a "Sephardic mental-
ity" regarding the welcoming of Jews of all observance levels into
Anshei Shalom:

> In Afghanistan, or Sephardic, there is no separa-
> tion of Reform, Conservative, Orthodox. If you are
> a Jew—Reform, Orthodox—you belong to one *shul*
> [synagogue] . . . That's the way tradition has been in
> Afghanistan, too, all over the Sephardic community.
> There is no separation, "Oh, you're not Orthodox,
> don't come to my *shul*;" there is no such thing. It's a
> practice in the whole Oriental mentality...But in [*sic*]
> Ashkenazim, I don't think this probably would be
> accepted. We [Afghan Jews] don't separate ourselves if
> you're religious, not religious.[54]

This interviewee revealed his understanding of different Jewish
movements, as well as his absorption of Ashkenazi phrases. He
explained that Ashkenazi synagogues, divided along sectarian
lines, have stricter demarcations regarding the types of religious
observances present in the synagogue. Using words like "*shul*,"
the Yiddish term for "synagogue," he illustrated his view of
Afghanistan as part of the larger Sephardic world.

The Afghan Jewish interviewees held differing opinions about
whether their recent identity as Sephardic Jews was a negative or
positive development. Some, particularly those involved in Anshei
Shalom, disliked calling themselves "Sephardic" precisely because
they sought to preserve their unique identities as Afghan Jews. One
former president of Anshei Shalom, for example, opposed the use
of "Sephardic" in the synagogue's documents:

> In the bylaws of Anshei Shalom . . . it's Sephardic Afghan
> *minhagim* [customs] according to Shulhan Arukh . . . I
> don't know why they put Sephardic, they should've just
> put Afghan *minhagim*. You know what, because at that

> time they gave us a lawyer to do it. It was Sephardic,
> no other *kehilot* [congregations] were on the map.
> And we are not Sephardic. Afghans are not Sephardic.
> Afghans, Bukharians, Persians, Iraqis—we are *Mizrahim*
> [Easterners] . . . Because at that time . . . who did it, he
> only knew Ashkenazi and he only knew Sephardic. He
> didn't know anything else. He didn't know it existed
> anything else [*sic*]. Ashkenazi was European and every-
> body else was lumped into Sephardic.[55]

He reported, in short, that the consulting lawyer and not the congregants produced the Sephardic terminology in the synagogue's
bylaws. Criticizing how an American Jew automatically considered
non-European Jews as Sephardic, this interviewee preferred to use
the more specific word *Mizrahim*, or (Middle) Easterners, to refer
to Jews from Central Asia and the Middle East.

Despite his concerns, the majority of participants expressed neither alarm nor approval regarding the growing identity of Afghans
as Sephardic Jews. The term *Mizrahim* was unfamiliar to other
interviewees raised in Afghanistan. One interviewee from Kabul
said that the expression *Mizrahi* "is not popular[ly] known."[56] This
label also may offend those who lived in Israel for an extended
period of time, since Ashkenazi Jews in Israel often utilized this
term to distinguish themselves from their darker-skinned brethren who were newer arrivals to the country.[57] Rather than favor
the *Mizrahi* label, most interviewees of Afghan Jewish descent
felt ambivalent about the Sephardic identification and viewed it
as inevitable in the United States. While they desired to maintain
their unique customs, such as their cuisine and celebratory tunes,
they did not feel that the added Sephardic identity diminished
their native Afghan one.

On a practical level, these cognitive changes—such as absorbing a new Sephardic identity—will likely result in some loss of
Afghan Jewish traditions. One significant consequence already,
for instance, has been the near disappearance of the Afghan dialect of Judeo-Persian, the primary language spoken by Jews in
Afghanistan. An interviewee from Kabul said he regretted that the

broader Afghan Jewish community in the United States did not teach Judeo-Persian to their children:

> Afghans . . . don't teach their children their own language. . . Like in [sic] Ashkenazim, they teach their children Yiddish, their mother tongue. We did not teach our children our mother language . . . [The] Persian community, Russian community—they teach their children their own mother language. We did not. We did not emphasize, we did not bother with it, we let it go.[58]

Because of the Afghan Jewish community's small size and the subsequent large number of marriages between Afghan and non-Afghan Jews, Judeo-Persian is now almost completely foreign to the children of Afghan Jews. The absence of Judeo-Persian then makes it more difficult to maintain an Afghan identity. Other Afghan Jewish customs also might vanish in the future without a conscious effort to retain them. The loss of Afghan Jews' specific dialect and the fading of their distinct ethnic identity thus have a cyclical effect on one another.

Triggers of Identity Alteration

Afghan Jews today identify as "Orthodox" and "Sephardic" primarily because most Jews in the United States are Ashkenazi and utilize these terms. Only 250,000 to 300,000 of the 5.2 to 6.4 million Jews living in America are not Ashkenazi.[59] The above range of the size of American Jewry varies so much because there is no consensus on the methods that studies should use to count the Jewish population.[60] The American Sephardi Federation lists 139 non-Ashkenazi congregations in the United States, which comprise less than four percent of the total number of American synagogues.[61] Clearly, "Ashkenazim form the vast majority of American Jews."[62]

The longer Afghan Jews have been in America, the more the norms of Ashkenazi Jewry have shaped their religious and ethnic identities. In the United States, Afghan Jews came to affiliate specifically with Orthodoxy as opposed to another wing of Judaism because they viewed Orthodoxy as analogous to the religious observance practiced in Afghanistan. They also considered themselves "Sephardic" rather than "Ashkenazi" simply because American Jews commonly used the label of "Sephardic" to describe Jewish populations from outside of Europe, even though these non-Ashkenazi Jewish communities hailed from many different countries and observed diverse customs.

The increasing enrollment of Afghan Jewish children in Ashkenazi schools also contributed to the growth of the "Orthodox" and "Sephardic" identifications. Once parents who wanted their children to remain observant sent them to Jewish day schools, which had large Ashkenazi student bodies, Afghan Jewish children started absorbing the notion of separate Jewish movements and brought these ideas home. One young interviewee described a circular influence in her upbringing. Her parents enrolled her in Orthodox schools because the family already espoused similar religious values, but constant attendance in such educational institutions reinforced the idea of a distinctly "Orthodox" life. She and the other young interviewee, who both attended Anshei Shalom, went to (different) Orthodox day schools, high schools, and then yeshivas in Israel for a year of study prior to college. She described herself as "modern Orthodox;" the other young interviewee called himself "an observant, Orthodox Jew." Both also said they were "Sephardic Jews," all the while stressing their families' specific countries of origin. Children and their parents from non-Ashkenazi backgrounds tend to influence each other to view themselves along Ashkenazi Jewish paradigms.[63]

These changes to Afghan Jews' identities reflect common immigrant experiences that are *not* limited to Jewish immigrant populations. Afghan Jews' consideration of themselves as part of the wider Sephardic world mirrors the process of ethnicization, by which immigrants alter their particular, localized affiliations from "the old country" to broader identifications. In just one example, Chinese arrivals to the United States during the 19th century engaged in open hostility with one another because of tensions between the "Hakka" and "Punti" groups. But over time, they came to view themselves along similar "Chinese" cultural and ethnic lines. So too, European Jewish immigrants in America often originally self-identified according to their city, rather than their country, of origin. Yet with the passing of generations, they placed themselves under the more general national categories of Italian Jewry, German Jewry, etc.[64] With such a small population, Afghan Jews did not identify themselves by their native cities, like Herat or Kabul, either in Afghanistan *or* in the United States. But their recent propensity to view themselves as "Sephardic" alongside their Afghan identity, whether in official synagogue documents or informal conversations, parallels a recurrent pattern among immigrants of assuming a new self-concept that is part of a larger ethnic group.

The causes underlying Afghan Jews' new identities are also similar to the forces behind the general process of ethnicization. Ethnicization tends to result from the host society ascribing immigrants to broad categories, often because of difficulties in understanding differences between ethnic groups.[65] Immigrants, in turn, frequently accept these designated identities from the dominant culture as they fear hardships, such as "prejudice and hostility," from the majority population.[66] Immigrant communities, Jewish and non-Jewish alike, want to feel welcome in and understood by their new country. Though many still desire to retain traditions from their native lands, they also yearn to be recognized as part of their new society. It is simpler to assume the identity that the majority impresses upon them rather than enforce or explain the nuances between ethnic and religious groups, such as Jews from different areas in the Middle East. In the case of Afghan Jews, they absorbed the "Sephardic" designation from American Jews unfamiliar with the diverse locales and customs that distinguish non-Ashkenazi Jews from one another. For Afghans and other Jews from countries outside Europe, identifying as "Sephardic" provides a frame of reference for the American Jewish majority.

While Afghan Jews' identity changes only began with their arrival in the United States, it was actually in their native country that they started observing certain Jewish practices not indigenous to Afghanistan. Jews in Afghanistan during the modern period utilized prayer books mailed from Jerusalem that were written in the *Edot Ha-mizrah nusah* [the prayer version of Middle Eastern Jewish communities]. We do not know exactly when these shipments started or whether the *Edot Ha-mizrah nusah* replaced an earlier Afghan Jewish prayer version. Still, it is likely that a specific Afghan *nusah* once existed. How much this Afghan Jewish *nusah* may have deviated from the prayer versions of other Central Asian or Middle Eastern Jewish communities at the time is further unknown. In Afghanistan, the Jews welcomed using the *Edot Ha-mizrah nusah* because of its strong tie to the Holy Land and the Jews living there, who also utilized this prayer version. The *Edot Ha-mizrah nusah* thus reinforced feelings of Jewish unity and nationhood for the isolated Afghan Jewish community. Once they arrived in America, Afghan Jews' use of the *Edot Ha-mizrah nusah* continued to link them to Israel, as well as to other non-Ashkenazi communities in the United States who prayed in the same *nusah*. The fact that Jews in Afghanistan used the *Edot Ha-mizrah nusah* at all shows that they accepted, even before coming to America, certain non-Afghan Jewish practices that strengthened their bond to the wider Jewish world. This openness to more prevalent Jewish traditions likely facilitated Afghan Jews' later absorption of the "Orthodox" and "Sephardic" labels in America, where these new identifications enabled them to affiliate with bigger Jewish communities. It was in Afghanistan that the Jews became somewhat familiarized with observing practices stemming from outside their country of origin and which connected them to larger, more recognizable Jewish groups.[67]

Fundamentally, the most significant challenges Afghan Jews still face in maintaining a distinct identity in the United States result from their sheer lack of numbers. With such a small community, identifying as "Sephardic" along with countless other Middle Eastern and Central Asian Jews sharply augments Afghan Jews' population size. Being part of larger Sephardic Jewry allows Afghan Jews to join a more widely known group in the predominantly Ashkenazi American Jewish community.

Afghan Jewry vis-à-vis the
Iranian Jewish Community in America

Nowadays, the preservation of ethnic identity also somewhat concerns, but does not threaten as strongly, the tens of thousands of Iranian Jews in the United States. Some of them sense that their distinct Persian customs might eventually disappear, as they "believe that their Iranian culture is a thing of the past and that they must look toward the future." [68] Yet overall, many Iranian Jews still maintain deep connections with and positive memories of their country of origin, which spur the active promotion of their heritage. Most came to America because of the Iranian Revolution in 1979, over three decades after Afghanistan's Jewish community began to emigrate. [69] The first Iranian Jews to arrive in the United States felt a firm attachment to Iran despite the chaos from which they had fled, for "Iranian Jews frequently had one eye on this country [America] and the other on Iran; they sought temporary refuge from what they regarded as a time-limited resurgence of Islamic fundamentalism." [70] The exception seems to be the Meshedi Jewish community and its resentment toward Iran, as the pain of the forced conversions in the 19th century remains a focal point in Meshedi communal memory. [71] Despite many Jews' fondness for their native Iran, it is unclear whether any moved back. Given that country's unstable political situation, it is unlikely that many Jews permanently returned to Iran after 1979. [72] It is even more improbable that *any* Jews went back to Afghanistan after the founding of the State of Israel and the later Soviet and Taliban incursions. None of the Afghan Jewish interviewees expressed a wish to live there again; one participant from Kabul said that he "has no feeling for Afghanistan." [73]

Iranian Jews' nostalgia for their country of origin, coupled with the large size of their community, has significantly aided their efforts in preserving their customs and ethnic identities. They founded multiple synagogues and organizations devoted to maintaining their traditions and to easing their acculturation to America; there are fourteen Iranian Jewish organizations in Los Angeles alone. [74] In New York, certain Jewish day schools near Iranian Jewish communities have predominantly Iranian student bodies. This allows for an easier observance of Iranian Jewish traditions, as Iranian students have peers from similar backgrounds and school educators have become acquainted with the practices of the children's families.[75] Congregation Anshei Shalom, meanwhile, remains the sole organizational connection among Afghan Jews in the entire United States. The fact that just a single Jewish institution focuses upon Afghan heritage underscores the community's small numbers as well as the difficulty in promoting Afghan Jewish traditions.

Moreover, Iranian Jews in America, unlike Afghan Jews, maintain a high rate of in-marriage within their community.[76] It is even common to wed someone whose family hails from the same city in Iran. Tehrani Jews, for instance, who consider themselves as the urban elite, do not have warm relations with Meshedis, who hold the forced conversions of 1839 as the distinguishing experience of their community.[77] Whether in California or New York, the two main American centers of Iranian Jewry, Jews from certain areas of Iran essentially created enclaves where they segregated themselves from Iranians of other cities and from non-Iranians even more severely.[78] Afghan Jews, in contrast, do not differentiate between Jews from various Afghan cities. In America, Afghan Jews almost never marry each other simply because the community is quite small. One couple from Kabul said that their (American) daughter did marry a man of Afghan Jewish descent—her friend from their synagogue—but her parents themselves emphasized that this was an atypical and rare occurrence.[79] Unlike Iranian Jews, many of whom call themselves "Tehrani," "Meshedi," etc.,[80] Afghanistan's Jews share an "Afghan" identity, one not localized to particular regions within the country.[81]

The many in-marriages among Iranian Jews facilitate the continuation of Judeo-Persian as a spoken language—another major difference from Afghan Jewry. One researcher examining New York's Iranian Jewish population reported in 2004 that a significantly high ninety-seven percent of his study's participants, mostly from Great Neck, Long Island, "spoke Farsi [Persian]."[82] The frequent marriages between Iranian Jews are evidently instrumental in enabling both an Iranian identity and the Judeo-Persian language to be passed down to their children—many who feel particularly tied to the Iranian city from which their parents came. Even the children of Meshedi Jews, who do not favorably remember Iran, still retain strong ethnic bonds, for "young community members who identify first as American always add it as merely another layer to their Mashadi [sic] identity."[83] The children of Afghan Jews, meanwhile, do not identify as Afghan—let alone as from a specific city—because most were born in the United States, and also since their parents married non-Afghan Jews.

Considering their tiny numbers and the fact that many came to think of themselves as "Sephardic," one might expect that Afghan Jews also eventually viewed themselves as part of the Iranian Jewish community. But Afghan Jews in America, as in Afghanistan, do not identify as Iranian. Nor, probably due to their disparate sizes, do Afghans share one community in the United States with Iranian Jews. The insular Iranian Jewish community has numerous synagogues and establishments from which Afghan Jews remain apart. Conversely, Iranians do not feel any need to join the Afghan synagogue in New York. Iranian Jews were never one of the many groups, such as Bukharians, Syrians, and Israelis, that attended Congregation Anshei Shalom. None of the interviewees from Afghanistan once called themselves a Persian or Iranian Jew, even while they continuously stressed the cultural and historical connections among Afghan, Iranian, and Bukharian Jews. I return to a telling statement from one Jewish woman from Herat, who remarked in our interview, "They're different; they're Meshedi. We're Afghan."[84] Despite a similar religious heritage from their respective countries of origin, Afghan Jews and Iranian Jews did not, and presently still do not, maintain the same ethnic identity.

The Future of Afghan Jewry in America

Given the minuscule size of the Afghan Jewish community, its synagogue in the United States could play an essential role for Afghan Jews in preserving their cultural and religious traditions. Since their community only has Anshei Shalom as a specific Afghan Jewish institution, their synagogue—which could potentially unite or split Afghan Jews—is thus heightened in importance as a connector to one another as well as to their past.

The pattern of Afghan Jewry's ethnic identity alteration, furthermore, will likely hold true for most other Jewish communities in America—regardless of their country of origin. The longer Jews reside in the United States, the more they and especially their children probably will associate along polar lines as either "Ashkenazi" or "Sephardic" Jews. Nowadays, German and Polish Jews and their descendants rarely introduce themselves as such; rather, they commonly self-identify as "Ashkenazi" or "European" Jews. Similarly, Afghans, Iranians, and other Jews from Central Asia and the Middle East living in America often call themselves "Sephardic" Jews, even though the term literally points to Spanish Jewry alone. The "Sephardic" identification is possibly beneficial as a unifying force for various Jewish communities who, like many Ashkenazi Jews, might then share the same prayer version, foods, and customs. Yet some fear that the "Ashkenazi" and "Sephardic" labels create overly simplistic categories that connote a divisive sense of "the other." And precisely because these terms are so broad, they inherently threaten the likelihood that Jewish communities from different countries might be able to retain their specific traditions. Still, given that the adoption of these titles appears inevitable, they also potentially could promote harmony within each Ashkenazi or Sephardic contingent, bringing together peoples from a multitude of different locales and cultures to affiliate under a single, new identity.

AFGHAN JEWRY PAST AND PRESENT

Few who venture to Afghanistan are aware that a Jewish community once resided there as early as the medieval period and possibly even biblical times. That Afghanistan ever had a Jewish population remains widely unknown among both scholars and the general public. Yet thankfully, the history of Afghan Jewry has drawn somewhat more interest in recent years because of the global political focus on Afghanistan. Since 2002, cultural foundations have restored the handful of Jewish structures in the country. Miraculously all of Afghanistan's five synagogues still stand; the Taliban, for unidentified reasons, did not destroy them. Kabul is home to a solitary synagogue, built in 1966, with the last Jew in Afghanistan living inside the building. Sadly the media have sometimes utilized his story as a source of mockery, rather than as a cause for reflection upon the near disappearance of certain Jewish communities.[1] Four synagogue structures, meanwhile, remain in Herat, once the largest center of Afghan Jewish life. As of 2005, the Aga Khan Trust for Culture has been successfully renovating all of the Herati synagogues, clearing them of garbage and debris.[2] Restorers have even found a *mikvah* [ritual bath] within the Mullah Yoav synagogue, located near a Jewish cemetery. The restoration in Herat endeavors to fulfill its double goals of "conservation and social development" as workers strive to preserve the buildings and to simultaneously create much-needed educational and prayer space for Muslims in this overcrowded city.[3] The Mullah Yoav synagogue and two others are now utilized as Muslim schools, and the fourth synagogue is used as a mosque.[4] The archaeologists and restorers involved know about the buildings' Jewish past, but the children attending elementary school there do not.[5] Though these contemporary functions of former Jewish sacred spaces are less than ideal, it is important that the buildings be kept intact, and receive deserved attention as a significant part of Afghanistan's religious and social history.

A fundamental piece of the Jews' story in Afghanistan was their relationship with the Muslim populace, which, throughout the generations, remained generally peaceful. The Jewish community particularly enjoyed professional cooperation with Afghans in mercantile trade. This tolerance of the Jews resulted partially from Islamic law itself, which applied in all Muslim-controlled lands and not just in Afghanistan. Islam's classification of Jews as *dhimmi*s, a specific "protected" class of monotheistic peoples that included Christians, enabled *dhimmi*s to practice their religions in exchange for certain restrictions and extra tax payments. But in Afghanistan specifically, Muslim openness toward the Jews largely derived from shared communal practices and myths. Muslim and Jewish sources, as well as foreign travelers to Afghanistan, describe how the Jews and the Afghan Pashtuns, who were Sunnis, both traced their lineage to the Ten Lost Tribes of Israel. As the biggest ethnic group in Afghanistan, the Pashtuns' perpetuation of the tale meant that the majority of the country's inhabitants believed they descended from the Jewish people. Even Afghanistan's very name supposedly stems from a Jewish figure according to Afghan lore, which alleges that the country was named after Afghana, a grandson of King Saul in Muslim tradition.[6] For the Jews, the story of the Ten Lost Tribes connected them all the way to the First Temple period, the Holy Land, and world Jewry. This legend stayed central to the Pashtuns' understandings of their origins at least until the mid-20th century, when Afghan nationalists began asserting that Afghanistan's Muslims originated from the Aryan people.[7] For centuries beforehand, Pashtuns claimed that they *and* the Jews shared the lost Israelites as ancestors, while Jews held that they alone stemmed from the Ten Tribes. The Pashtuns' belief in the legend created an underlying respect for the Jews. Pashtuns expressed pride over their Jewish roots and even preferred their Jewish "brothers" over Iran's Shiite Muslims, whom the Sunni Pashtuns in Afghanistan loathed.[8]

While some researchers and explorers still conduct far-flung attempts to discover descendants of the Ten Lost Tribes,[9] the legend's real significance, I believe, lies in its emotional impact. It is much more relevant to examine *why* a particular communal story lasts for generations, rather than try in vain to ascertain its veracity. We cannot determine whether communities or individuals actually descended from the lost Israelites. For Afghan Jewry, the legend survived partly because of its biblical origin and partly due to its prevalence among many Sunni Pashtuns, with whom Jews interacted closely in business. The Jewish and Muslim communities' pride in the story came from each group's conviction that it had inherited an ancient lineage. Especially for the Jews in isolated Afghanistan, this legend provided a firm bond to Jewish nationhood and a wellspring of hope for a return someday to Zion.

The endurance of the tale of the Ten Lost Tribes also reflects a culture of oral transmission among Afghans, Jews and non-Jews alike, which stemmed from low literacy rates among the general population and the late arrival of the printing press (around 1871) to Afghanistan.[10] In the Jewish community, folktales in particular served as a significant mode to entertain *and* to convey religious and ethical values. Many stories, such as "The Princess Who Became a Garland of Flowers" and "A Treasure from Heaven," which appear before Chapters 1 and 2, respectively, emphasize devotion to God and the search for piety over materialistic wealth. Others, including "The Lamp That Passed" preceding Chapter 4, indicate that honesty and integrity must be maintained in secular, financial realms, not just religious ones.

Still other folktales—like "The Jewish Shepherd," which introduces Chapter 3—mirror the Afghan Jewish community's constant apprehension about mixing closely with non-Jews. This cautious approach toward Muslims remained despite the general tolerance that prevailed between the two populations. Outside of the professional sphere, Afghan Jews actively avoided social interactions with their non-Jewish counterparts, fearing bodily harm as well as threats to Jewish observance. The majority of Afghan Jews in the 20th century opposed changes that would bring them closer to secularism and the non-Jewish world, especially in regards to education. As early as the 1920s, the Jewish community rejected the Afghan government's efforts to integrate Jewish youngsters into the public school system. In such cases, Jewish families primarily dreaded that their children might Islamicize or encounter violence from Muslim students and teachers. Most Jewish elders also refused to allow their family members to attend the Jewish school established by a *shaliah* [emissary of Zion] from Palestine in 1927; in that instance, they were concerned about decreased Jewish observance.

When designing new Jewish structures, too, the community was wary of drawing unwanted attention. During the building of Kabul's new synagogue in 1966, community leaders instructed that an adornment of small Jewish stars on the synagogue's railings and outside walls should be intelligible only to those standing close to it. Some Muslims might perchance recognize the Stars of David, but the synagogue was purposely engineered so that, from a distance, it appeared to contain nondescript geometric designs. Certainly none of the synagogues, either in Herat or Kabul, boasted large Jewish symbols on their facades.[11] While Jews in Afghanistan did not feel the need to hide their religion, they were neither comfortable nor confident in asserting it.

Yet within the communal majority's steadfast resistance to secularization, a limited amount of modernity altered the views of individuals—particularly men—regarding traditional Jewish education. Afghan Jewish men's frequent business travels across Central Asia, the Soviet Union, and Europe exposed them to more progressive ideas that they brought back home. Several families in both Herat and Kabul sought out private secular education for their sons in order to advance their professional futures— hiring tutors so that Jewish boys could learn how to write in Persian script and even in the English language. Jewish men, who attended *heder* from a young age, enjoyed much higher literacy rates than the rest of the Afghan population. Certain *heders* also taught mathematics. Meanwhile, most Jewish women in Afghanistan, like almost all women there, were illiterate and relegated nearly full-time to the home. But in Kabul, education for Jewish girls improved during the 1960s. The government required the city's children, including Jews, to enroll in public schools, which both Jewish boys and girls in Kabul then attended. More significantly, some Jewish families in Kabul chose to send their daughters to *heder* with the boys during that same decade. Girls in *heder* learned how to read the Bible and Hebrew prayers. Though these changes only occurred in the final years that many Jews still lived in Afghanistan, they reveal that part of Kabul's Jewish community began to view girls' education—including their Jewish education—as a more formal affair that should contain textual instruction.

Regarding the role of Jewish women, even more surprising than Kabul's girls attending *heder* was an Afghan Jewish man's admission in his memoir that he had wanted his daughter to receive a Jewish divorce in the 1950s. The author expressed his deep distress from watching his child suffer in an abusive marriage, even though she herself preferred to remain wedded. She considered matrimony first and foremost as a means of providing financial protection for the future. The author's daughter resolved to stay with her spouse rather than risk social ostracism as a young divorced woman in Herat's Jewish community. All Afghan women, regardless of their religion, were by and large expected to remain with their husbands no matter the circumstances. That is precisely the reason why the author's concern for his daughter's personal fulfillment over her marital status is so unexpected. The author was part of a tiny minority among the Jewish community, as well as Afghans in general, who would advocate divorce over unhappiness. Still, it is possible that others shared a similar outlook.

These educational and attitudinal shifts remained limited in scope since they were mostly confined to the private sphere of Jewish spaces. Tutors taught English to Jewish boys in their families' homes. And *heder* took place inside the synagogue. When Jewish girls in Kabul started attending *heder*, their families sent them to a known and comforting sacred place. Under the protective eyes of community members, Jewish families became somewhat more open to the idea of exposing their children to secular subjects. Parents opposed sending children to unfamiliar public schools and the inevitable social mingling between Jewish and Muslim youth there. The Jews did not necessarily fear intermarriage, an almost unheard-of occurrence in Afghanistan, but they worried about Jewish children being physically harmed or even abducted. Only under government decree in the 1960s did Jewish families in Kabul reluctantly send their children to Afghan public schools.

The 1960s, indeed, ushered a wave of modernity into Afghanistan as a whole, especially within its more tolerant capital city of Kabul. Certain changes within the Jewish community, especially in Kabul, directly reflect the political climate of that time. Muhammed Zahir Shah's new constitution in 1964 increased educational and economic opportunities for women, in part through the establishment of more schools. In a 2009 interview to CNN, Afghan Muslim women who used to live in Kabul reported that they wore miniskirts openly in the city streets during the 1960s and 1970s.[12] In this light, it is unsurprising that the government demanded that its Jewish population, including girls, in Kabul attend public schools to receive formal education. These changes were harder to implement in cities farther from Kabul, like Herat, where the government could not exercise its power as strongly. If the Jewish community had stayed in Afghanistan after the 1960s, by which time the majority had emigrated, more Jews in Kabul and perhaps in Herat, too, may have supported improving Jewish women's education as long as they remained devoted to their traditional roles within the home and family.

After leaving Afghanistan, most of the hundreds of Jews who went to the United States settled in New York, which is still home to the sole Afghan synagogue, Congregation Anshei Shalom, in the entire diaspora. The Jews' experiences in Afghanistan explain much about their later acculturation to America, particularly within the synagogue and educational realms. Afghan Jews sought to integrate their knowledge of tribal systems with the modern ideals of their new surrounding society. We see this in the *hevra*-style running of Anshei Shalom that continued to exist alongside

the democratization of the synagogue's governance. Jewish education in Afghanistan, which had little need to concern itself with
intermarriage or decreased observance, concentrated on practical applications of Jewish traditions. But many Afghan Jews,
upon arriving in the United States, were eager to Americanize
and became less observant than in their country of origin. These
new challenges to maintaining Afghan Jews' cultural and religious lifestyles thus necessitated some shifts in their synagogue's
purposes. Afghanistan's synagogues, also the location of *heder*,
instilled religious traditions, whereas Afghan Jews' synagogue
in America became a main center for enforcing ethnic identity.
Jewish day schools in the United States fulfilled the role of synagogues in Afghanistan as formal Jewish education became the
primary means of inculcating observance, with children spending
their days in dual-curriculum schools that taught both Jewish and
secular subjects.

The exposure to modernity in Afghanistan, furthermore, seems
to have been significant enough to facilitate the Jews' adaptation to
some American norms. Western influences in Afghanistan, including
the creation of a new national constitution, previously familiarized
Afghan Jews—especially those in Kabul—with certain democratic
ideas that they later embraced more fully in America when formal-
izing their synagogue's governance. Looking to American democracy as a model, Afghan Jewish leaders incorporated elections, a
presidency, and bylaws into their synagogue in New York.

Afghan Jewry's acculturation experiences in the United States,
as we have seen, occur quite commonly across immigrant groups—
Jews and non-Jews alike. Communities of different religions often
base their houses of worship's organizational systems on the
American government by forming a constitution and holding elections. The ethnicization process in America, moreover, touched
Afghan Jews along with German Jews, Eastern European Jews,
and countless other Jewish *and* non-Jewish communities. Many
immigrants from all religious and ethnic backgrounds initially pin-
point their origins to specific cities and later expand this identification to entire countries or even greater regions (i.e., "My family is

from Cairo" eventually becomes "My family is from Egypt" and then, "My family is from the Middle East").

Regarding Jewish identifications, ultimately most Jews in America widen their ethnic identity beyond particular countries to the much larger groups of "Ashkenazi" or "Sephardic" Jews. Afghan Jews' absorption of the new classifications of "Sephardic" and "Orthodox" allows them to be part of bigger Jewish bodies in the predominantly Ashkenazi American Jewish community. Afghán Jews' acceptance of these labels, utilized extensively by the American Jewish majority, thus provides a frame of reference for American Jews, since most are unfamiliar with the differences between Jewish communities from various lands in the Middle East and Central Asia. Even Iranian Jews who, unlike Afghan Jews, remain devoted to their specific native cities probably will consider themselves "Iranians" and then "Sephardic" the longer their families continue to reside in the United States. First-generation Iranians already care less than their parents whether Jews hail from different Iranian cities.[13] As time passes, more Afghan Jews and more Jews in America overall, regardless of their country of origin, likely will come to self-identify as either "Sephardic" or "Ashkenazi."

While the "Sephardic" label enables Afghans and many other Jews from Central Asia and the Middle East to attain a more well-known identity, such a broad categorization inherently hinders efforts to retain specific cultural and religious customs. For the Afghan Jewish community, the loss of Judeo-Persian is the most prominent example. Most Afghan Jews do not view the term "Sephardic" as a threat to their original Afghan identity. For those concerned about waning traditions, they tend to rely upon their synagogue, Anshei Shalom, to reinforce their cultural ties. Many other small Jewish communities, such as the Yemenite Jewish community in New York, also look to their synagogue as the chief mode of fortifying ethnic bonds.[14] When congregations are formed by Jews from a particular country, their synagogues play a vital role in strengthening and sustaining ethnic and cultural traditions, not just religious practices.

However, a significant factor distinguishing Afghan Jewry from other immigrant communities (both Jewish and non-Jewish) is the

absence of nostalgia among Afghan Jews for their country of origin. Almost none of the interviewees expressed fondness or regard
for Afghanistan. It seems that the legend of the Ten Lost Tribes
mostly connected Jews to Afghanistan while they resided there,
providing them with a sense of comfort that they were part of
world Jewry and linked to the Land of Israel. Once Afghan Jews
moved elsewhere and lived among larger Jewish populations, they
became less emotionally attached to the land of their birth. This
indifference toward Afghanistan is atypical of immigrant groups,
who often reminisce over "the old country" once leaving it. Many
immigrants of various religious and ethnic backgrounds feel tied
to their native lands.[15] One main reason Afghan Jews have not
maintained a shared nostalgic recollection for Afghanistan is that
they fortunately did not have to endure a major communal disas-
ter, which, for all its tragic results, tends to ignite a community's
conscious drive to remember its own history. Those with ties to
the Holocaust, and to a lesser extent the *Allahdad* [forced conversions in Meshed in 1839] and the *Farhud* [pogrom in Baghdad in
1941], are considerably more likely to create museums, courses,
and events that commemorate Jewish life during such times of persecution. While Afghanistan's Jews were not made to suffer a communal tragedy, the discriminatory decrees of the 1930s and 1940s
still caused many to leave without hesitation. Also, Afghanistan's
isolation from global advances and world Jewry deterred warm
sentiments from developing.

Their minimal romanticism regarding Afghanistan also helps
explain the relative quickness with which Afghan Jews in America
have subconsciously absorbed the "Orthodox" and "Sephardic"
identities. Most interviewees did not feel that their new affiliations
endangered their Afghan Jewish heritage or customs. In a circular pattern, this indifference toward "the old country" facilitates
the acceptance of a larger ethnic identity—such as "Sephardic"—
which then results in reduced nostalgia toward one's native land.

Though some Jews from Middle Eastern and Central Asian
countries dislike calling themselves "Sephardic" because they trace
their roots to the First Temple period, not medieval Spain, many

feel that the "Sephardic" affiliation's significant benefits—like allowing smaller Jewish groups to share a unified, more recognizable identity within the American Jewish population—essentially outweigh concerns that particular traditions could fade. Whether Jewish communities in the United States have European origins, like Danish Jews, or Middle Eastern backgrounds, like Iraqi Jews, all are more likely to identify as either "Ashkenazi" or "Sephardic" with the passing years.

Afghan Jewry in the United States today remains a community in flux, as if facing a crossroads. One path represents the desire to engage in—and be understood by—American society *and* American Jewry. Another path signifies observing unique customs from Afghanistan, which have become increasingly difficult to retain because there are simply few Afghan Jews in the United States to keep them. Afghan Jews, like many other immigrant communities of all religions and all ethnicities, want to secularize without fully losing their traditions. By preserving their history and practices, Afghan Jews can integrate their past into their present, and thereby strengthen the commemoration of Jewish life in Afghanistan.

NOTES

NOTE ON GEOGRAPHICAL TERMS

1 Clayton R. Koppes, "Captain Mahan, General Gordon, and the Origins of the Term 'Middle East,'" *Middle Eastern Studies* Vol. 12, No. 1 (1976), p. 96.

2 Roger Adelson, *London and the Invention of the Middle East: Money, Power, and War, 1902–1922* (New Haven: Yale University Press, 1995), p. 25.

3 Devin DeWeese, "Islam in Central Asia," *Encyclopedia of Islam and the Muslim World*, ed. Richard C. Martin, Vol. 1 (New York: Macmillan Reference USA, 2004), pp. 132–138.

INTRODUCTION

1 This encounter occurred at Columbia University in February 2009.

2 Erich Brauer, "The Jews of Afghanistan," *Jewish Social Studies* Vol. 4, No. 2 (1942), p. 122.

3 "Afghanistan," *Encyclopedia Britannica* (2008).

4 Some notable exceptions are Vartan Gregorian, *The Emergence of Modern Afghanistan: Politics of Reform and Modernization, 1880–1946* (Stanford: Stanford University Press, 1969), and Milan Hauner, *India in Axis Strategy: Germany, Japan and Indian Nationalists in the Second World War* (Stuttgart, Germany: Klett-Cotta, 1981). Gregorian and Hauner both explain the important role that Jews and other religious minorities, such as Hindus, played in Afghanistan's mercantile trade and overall economy. See Gregorian, *The Emergence of Modern Afghanistan*, p. 315, and Hauner, *India in Axis Strategy*, p. 86. Still, neither author discusses the Afghan Jewish community as a separate subject.

5 For instance, see Ken Blady, *Jewish Communities in Exotic Places* (New Jersey: Jason Aronson, Inc., 2000), p. 205, and Reuben Kashani, *The Jews of Afghanistan* [English translation] (Jerusalem: Reuben Kashani, 2002), p. 27.

6 For example, see Bentzion Yehoshua Raz, *Mi-nidhei Yisrael Li-anusei Meshed Bi-iran* [From the Ten Lost Tribes of Israel to Meshed's Forced Converts in Iran] (Jerusalem: Bialik Institute, 1992). Also see No'am Baraam Ben Yoseff, ed., *Brides and Betrothals: Jewish Wedding Rituals in Afghanistan* (Jerusalem: The Israel Museum, 1998), p. 22; "It is hard to point to any evidence of secularist tendencies in the community even in

the case of individuals. Except for a few large exporters who traveled to foreign countries and became acquainted with modern lifestyles, Afghan Jewry was hardly exposed at all to processes of modernization (at least until the 1930s) and strenuously opposed any attempt to reform its educational institutions, thus remaining a very conservative community."

7 Ben Yoseff, ed., *Brides and Betrothals*, p. 22.

8 For more on Afghan Jewry in Israel, see Israel Mishael, *Bein Afghanistan Li-eretz Yisrael* [Between Afghanistan and the Land of Israel] (Jerusalem, 1981).

CHAPTER 1

1 This is an abridged version of the folktale based on the full English translation in Harold Schwartz, *Miriam's Tambourine: Jewish Folktales from around the World* (New York: Seth Press, 1984), pp. 135–140. For the full version in Hebrew, see Zevulun Kort, ed., *Bat Ha-melekh Shehafkha Li-ezer Prahim* [The Princess Who Became a Garland of Flowers] (Tel Aviv: Yehudit, 1967).

2 Schwartz, *Miriam's Tambourine*, p. 366.

3 Another interpretation of the fairytale holds that the princess and the maid represent Eve and Lillith, respectively, two figures who symbolize the good and evil facets of womankind. See Schwartz, *Miriam's Tambourine*, p. 366.

4 In one metaphorical translation of Song of Songs, for example, the groom's search for his bride represents God's yearning for a closer relationship with the Jewish people. See Solomon B. Freehof, "The Song of Songs: A General Suggestion," *The Jewish Quarterly Review* Vol. 39, No. 4 (1949), pp. 397–402.

5 Louis Rabinowitz, "Ten Lost Tribes," *Encyclopedia Judaica* 19 (2007), pp. 639–640.

6 See Kings II 17:6, "In the ninth year [of the reign of] Hosea, the king of Assyria captured Samaria and exiled Israel to Assyria, and he settled them in Halah, in Habor, by the Ghozan River, and in the cities of Media." Also see Chronicles I 5:26, "And the God of Israel stirred up the spirit of Pul king of Assyria and the spirit of Tillegathpilnesser, king of Assyria, and he led away the Reuvenites, the Gadites, and half the tribe of Manasseh into exile, bringing them to Halah, Habor, and Harah and to the Ghozan River, until this day." Also see Kings II 18:11.

7 Rabinowitz, "Ten Lost Tribes," pp. 639–640. While the tribes' fate can never be proven, Rabinowitz writes that "in general it can be said that they disappeared from the stage of history."

8 Tudor Parfitt, "Bene Menashe," *Encyclopedia Judaica* 3 (2007), p. 340.

9 Shalvah Weil, "Ethiopian Jews," *Encyclopedia of the Modern Middle East and North Africa* 2 (New York: 2004), pp. 786–788.

10 Emanuela Semi, Howard Lenhoff, Steven Kaplan, and E. Semi, "Beta Israel," *Encyclopedia Judaica* 3 (2007), pp. 499–509. On February 9,

1973, Ovadiah Yosef, a leading Sephardic rabbi in Israel, declared in a letter to Ovadiah Hazi, a former spokesman for Ethiopian Jews living in Israel, that "the Falashas ["wanderers," referring to Ethiopian Jews] are descendants of the Tribe of Israel who went southward to Ethiopia, and there is no doubt . . . that they are of the Tribe of Dan."

11 Cecil Roth, "Benjamin (ben Jonah) of Tudela," *Encyclopedia Judaica* 3 (2007), pp. 362–364.

12 A. Asher, trans., "The Itinerary of Benjamin of Tudela" (New York: Hakesheth Publishing Company, 1900), p. 129.

13 Marcus Nathan Adler, Introduction to *Massaot Shel R' Binyamin* [The Itinerary of Benjamin of Tudela] by Benjamin of Tudela (New York: Phillip Feldheim, Inc., 1907), xiii–xv. The differences in Asher's and Adler's translations result from their usage of different editions. Asher's translation (A), which first appeared in 1840, was based on two manuscripts: the Editio Princeps, printed in Constantinople in 1543, and the Ferrara Edition, printed by Abraham Usque in 1556. Meanwhile, Adler wrote a collated translation which marked the text variations from different manuscripts. The three complete texts he examined were the British Museum manuscript (BM), located in the British Museum and which some scholars date to the 13th century; the Roman manuscript (R), housed in the Cantanese library in Rome and dated to 1429–1430; and a manuscript owned by a Herr Epstein of Italy (E), who dates the text to the late 15th or early 16th centuries. In the passage about Nisapur, Asher was translating, *ki bi-arei* ("because in the cities"), while Adler translated R, which read, *ki yaish sham bi-harei* ("because there are in the mountains"). The translations result from the difference in one Hebrew letter; the presence of an *ayin* denotes "cities" while a *hey* denotes "mountain."

14 Ibid.; Asher, "Itinerary," p. 129. A. Asher omits the tribe of Asher, saying, "Four tribes of Israel . . . the tribe of Dan, that of S'bulun [*sic*] and that of Naphtali."

15 Walter J. Fischel, "The Jews of Medieval Iran from the 16th to the 18th Centuries: Political, Economic, and Communal Aspects," *Irano-Judaica* I (1982).

16 "Benjamin II," *Encyclopedia Judaica* 3 (2007), p. 356.

17 J.J. Benjamin II, *Eight Years in Asia and Africa: From 1846 to 1855* (Hanover: J.J. Benjamin II, 1859), p. 120.

18 Hilda Nissimi, *The Crypto-Jewish Mashadis: The Shaping of Religious and Communal Identity in Their Journey from Iran to New York* (Portland, Oregon: Sussex Academic Press, 2007), p. 61. Nissimi adds that the "important foundation myth" of the Lost Tribes among Meshedi Jewry "disappeared completely from communal memory" following the forced conversions in 1839; see p. 61. I doubt this sweeping claim that the legend totally vanished, but if Nissimi is correct, then Benjamin II probably did not interact with Meshedi Jews during his travels in Persia in 1851.

19 J.J. Benjamin II, *Eight Years*, p. 120.

20 Ibid. 159.

21 Ephraim Neumark, *Masah Bi-eretz Ha-kedem: Suria, Kurdistan, Aram Naharayim, Paras Vi-Asia Hamerkazit*, [Travel in the Eastern Land: Syria, Kurdistan, Iraq, Persia, and Central Asia] (Jerusalem: Epstein: 1860), p. 98 [Hebrew].

22 Ibid.

23 Yehoshua Raz, *Mi-nidhei Yisrael*, pp. 18-19.

24 Neumark, *Masah*, p. 99 [Hebrew].

25 Ibid.

26 The Safavid rulers of Iran (1502–1736) established Shia Islam as the country's religion. See Fischel, "The Jews of Medieval Iran," pp. 1–2.

27 Excerpt from interview with a Jewish man from Kabul (2), August 2007.

28 Ibid.

29 For the tombstone's discovery, see Walter J. Fischel, "The Rediscovery of the Medieval Jewish Community at Firuzkuh in Central Afghanistan," *Journal of the American Oriental Society* 85 (1965), p. 150. Fischel dates the tombstone to 1198 C.E. His dating came after scholar A. Dupont Sommer's alternative dating of the tombstone to 749 C.E. Sommer incorrectly thought that the tombstone's inscription was written in the Hebrew language. For more on Ghur and the Ghurid dynasty, see C.E. Bosworth, "Ghurids," *Encyclopaedia of Islam, Second Edition* Online (2010), eds. P. Bearman, Th. Bianquis, C.E. Bosworth, E. Van Donzel and W.P. Heinrichs, p. 1,099.

30 Fischel, "Firuzkuh," p. 150.

31 For more on the 8th century dating, see W.B. Henning, "The Inscriptions of Tang-I Azao," *Bulletin School of Oriental and African Studies* 20 (1957), pp. 335–342. Also see Fischel, "Firuzkuh," p. 150. Fischel writes that if the 8th century dating is correct, the tablet "would constitute the oldest document in the Judeo-Persian language written in Hebrew characters."

32 Yehoshua Raz, *Mi-nidhei Yisrael*, p. 69.

33 Andrea Bruno, "Notes on the Discovery of Hebrew Inscriptions in the Vicinity of the Minaret of Jam," *East and West (Rome)* 14 (1963), pp. 206–208. Also see Fischel, "Firuzkuh," p. 151.

34 Fischel, "Firuzkuh," p. 151. Fischel calls the Minaret of Jam "a remarkable monument, an edifice of exceeding beauty."

35 Ibid.

36 Bruno, "Minaret," pp. 207–208.

37 Eugen Rapp, *Die Jüdisch-perisch-hebräischen Inschriften aus Afghanistan* (1965), or the English translation, "The Judeo-Persian Hebrew Inscriptions of Afghanistan," *East and West (Rome)* 17 (1967), pp. 51–58. Rapp dates the earliest tombstone to 1115 C.E. My great thanks to Dr. Jonathan D. Sarna, Joseph H. & Belle R. Braun Professor of American Jewish History at Brandeis University, for helping me locate the English translation. Also see Fischel, "Firuzkuh," p. 152.

38 Bruno, "Minaret," p. 208.

39 Ibid.

40 Ibid.

41 Fischel, "Firuzkuh," p. 153.

42 Ibid. 152.

43 Ibid. 152, n. 24.

44 Walter J. Fischel, "The Jews of Central Asia (Khorasan) in Medieval Hebrew and Islamic Literature," *Historia Judaica* 7 (1945), p. 30.

45 Ibid; Yehoshua Raz, *Mi-nidhei Yisrael*, p. 35.

46 Afghanistan is mentioned as part of Khorasan in Fischel, "The Jews of Central Asia," p. 30; Fischel, "Firuzkuh," p. 148; Yehoshua Raz, *Mi-nidhei Yisrael*, p. 36; and Reuben Kashani, *Yehudei Afghanistan* [Hebrew] (Jerusalem: Reuben Kashani, 1975), p. 5.

47 For more on Jewish sources that discuss Khorasan, see Fischel, "The Jews of Central Asia," pp. 31–40; Fischel, "Firuzkuh," p. 148; Yehoshua Raz, *Mi-nidhei Yisrael*, pp. 35–38, 88–91.

48 For more on the exilarch's duties, see Jacob Neusner and Eliezer Bashan, "Exilarch," *Encyclopedia Judaica* 6 (2007), p. 600.

49 Fischel, "The Jews of Central Asia," p. 33. Natan Ha-bavli records that the conflict occurred during the days of an exilarch named Ukba. He explains that "the jurisdiction of Khorasan had in older times belonged to Pumbadita whence the *Dayanim* [rabbinical decisors] used to be sent thither, and all the tax on her revenues used to go to Pumbadita. [The exilarch] Ukba, however, wished . . . to take possession of her [Khorasan] and get hold of her revenue for himself alone, to the exclusion of Pumbadita."

50 Fischel, "The Jews of Central Asia," p. 33.

51 Ibid. 32.

52 Yehoshua Raz, *Mi-nidhei Yisrael*, p. 37. The specific blessing formula, translated into English, is, "Here you are betrothed to me with this ring according to the religious laws of Moses and Israel."

53 Interview with a Jewish man from Kabul (1), August 2007. He recounted the story of Hiwi al-Balkhi.

54 Judah Rosenthal, "Hiwi Al-Balkhi," *Encyclopedia Judaica* 9 (2007), p. 295.

55 Ibid.

56 Fischel, "Firuzkuh," p. 149.

57 Fischel, "The Jews of Central Asia," p. 36.

58 Fischel, "Firuzkuh," pp. 148–149. For more on non-Jewish sources that mention Khorasan, see Fischel, "The Jews of Central Asia," pp. 35, 38, and 40.

59 My knowledge of Muslim sources that discuss Khorasan is based upon Fischel's writings, "The Jews of Central Asia (Khorasan) in Medieval Hebrew and Islamic Literature" (1945) and "The Rediscovery of the Medieval Jewish Community at Firuzkuh in Central Afghanistan" (1965). Fischel cites medieval Muslim texts that I could not access directly. In Fischel's articles, it seems that these Muslim sources neither explicitly discuss nor exclude Afghan cities as part of Khorasan. But it

is possible that similar Muslim documents single out Afghan cities or regions in the context of Khorasan.

60 Norman A. Stillman, *The Jews of Arab Lands: A History and Source Book* (Philadelphia: The Jewish Publication Society, 1979), pp. 25–26.

61 For more on Moses Ibn Ezra, see "Ibn Ezra, Moses ben Jacob," *Encyclopedia Judaica* 9 (2007), p. 673.

62 In Walter J. Fischel, "Afghanistan," *Encyclopedia Judaica* 1 (2007), p. 432, and Kashani, *Yehudei Afghanistan* [Hebrew], p. 7, the earliest record of the number of Jews in an Afghan city comes from Ibn Ezra. Other researchers only cite Benjamin of Tudela when describing the size of the medieval Afghan Jewish population; see Yehoshua Raz, *Mi-nidhei Yisrael*, p. 27; and Blady, *Jewish Communities*, p. 199.

63 For Moses Ibn Ezra's description of the Jews, see Fischel, "Afghanistan," *Encyclopedia Judaica* 1 (2007), p. 432; and Kashani, *Yehudei Afghanistan* [Hebrew], p. 7. For more on the Ghaznavid Empire, see "Ghaznavid Dynasty," *Encyclopedia Britannica* Online (2010).

64 My translation is based on the text in Adler, *Massaot Shel R' Binyamin*, p. 54 [Hebrew].

65 Adler, "The Itinerary of Benjamin of Tudela," p. 93, n. 5. Meanwhile, Asher translates the city "Ghazna" as "Giva . . . on the banks of the Oxus," but he does not elaborate on the locations of these areas. See Asher, "The Itinerary," p. 128.

66 Asher, "The Itinerary," p. 128.

67 Adler, "The Itinerary of Benjamin of Tudela," p. 93. See n. 5 for his criticism of Asher's translation.

68 Fischel, "Afghanistan," p. 432; Kashani, *The Jews of Afghanistan* [English]; Blady, *Jewish Communities*, p. 199.

69 Kashani, *Yehudei Afghanistan* [Hebrew], p. 7. Kashani specifies that Benjamin of Tudela seems to derive his numbers from others' unconfirmed reports.

70 Fischel, "Afghanistan," *Encyclopedia Judaica* 1 (2007), p. 432.

71 Stephen Tanner, *Afghanistan* (New York: Da Capo Press, 2002), p. 81; Kashani, *Yehudei Afghanistan* [Hebrew], p. 8; Yehoshua Raz, *Mi-nidhei Yisrael*, p. 94.

72 "Islamic World," *Encyclopedia Britannica* (2007), p. 49.

73 Yehoshua Raz, *Mi-nidhei Yisrael*, p. 94.

74 Tanner, *Afghanistan*, pp. 81–82.

75 Ibid. 92.

76 Ibid. 96.

77 Fischel, "Afghanistan," *Encyclopedia Judaica* 1, p. 432. The map marks cities, including Balkh, that had Afghan Jewish settlements in the medieval period.

78 Fischel, *Firuzkuh*, p. 153.

79 Ibid. Fischel writes, "We may well assume that the Jewish community disappeared when the Mongol tribes...swept over this territory and destroyed their capital around 1222 A.D."

80 For a picture of the 1812 *ketubbah*, see the section of this book entitled "Photographs."

81 Joseph Wolff, *Narrative of a Mission to Bokhara in the Years 1843–1845* (Edinburgh: William Blackwood and Sons, 1848), p. 332; J.J. Benjamin II, *Eight Years*, p. 195; Walter J. Fischel, "The Jews of Persia, 1795–1940," *Jewish Social Studies* 12 (1950), p. 124; Rafael Patai, *Jadid al Islam* (Detroit: Wayne University Press, 1997), p. 51; Nissimi, *The Crypto-Jewish Mashadis.*

82 Wolff, *Narrative of a Mission to Bohkara*, p. 332. On the same day of a Muslim feast called "Bairam," a Jewish woman, heeding a Muslim physician's advice, killed a dog to wash her hands in its blood. A certain Muslim, "to whom the Jews previously had refused a present," heard of the Jewish woman's act and assembled many Muslims in a mosque. He decried killing the dog on the same day as the Muslim celebration, saying that "the Jews have derided our feast of Bairam," and called for retaliation.

83 Ibid.

84 Patai, *Jadid al Islam*, p. 51.

85 Wolff, *Narrative*, p. 332.

86 Mattatya Garji, *Korot Zemanim* [Chronicles of Afghanistan Jewry [*sic*] 1857–1904] (Jerusalem: Reuben Kashani, 1970), p. 12.

87 Book of Esther 3:13, 8:11.

88 Patai, *Jadid al Islam*, p. 51.

89 J.J. Benjamin II, *Eight Years*, p. 195.

90 Patai, *Jadid al Islam*, p. 59.

91 Fischel, "The Jews of Persia," p. 124.

92 Nissimi, *The Crypto-Jewish Mashadis*, p. 27.

93 Ibid.

94 Ibid. 27–28.

95 Ibid. 48; Patai, *Jadid al Islam*, p. 152; Louis Finkelstein, ed., *The Jews: Their History, Culture and Religion* (New York: Harper and Brothers, 1949), p. 1,177.

96 Yehoshua Raz, *Mi-nidhei Yisrael*, p. 105. Dilmani's account, recorded in 1945, is housed in the Central Zionist Archives in Jerusalem; see Patai, *Jadid al Islam*, p. 57.

97 Garji, *Korot Zemanim*, p. 12.

98 Nissimi, *The Crypto-Jewish Mashadis*, p. 48.

99 Garji himself left Meshed and therefore, may particularly favor those who also left Meshed to go to Herat. Still, it is likely that his views accurately reflect that more observant Jews left Meshed. See Nissimi, *The Crypto-Jewish Mashadis*, p. 48; Nissimi writes that "the entire group who fled to Herat is supposed to have done so on religious grounds, not wishing to embark on the 'double game' on the one hand, and wanting to stay true to their religion on the other."

100 Nissimi, *The Crypto-Jewish Mashadis*, p. 62; Finkelstein, *The Jews*, p. 1,177.

101 Neumark, *Masah*, pp. 87–88.

102 Yehoshua Raz, *Mi-nidhei Yisrael*, p. 109.

103 Ibid.

104 Neumark, *Masah*, p. 99.

105 For more on the 1857 Persia-Afghanistan war, see Muhammed Jamil Hanifi, *Historical and Cultural Dictionary of Afghanistan* (Metuchen, New Jersey: Scarecrow Press, 1976), p. 10.

106 Nissimi, *The Crypto-Jewish Mashadis*, p. 28; Patai, *Jadid al Islam*, p. 178.

107 Patai, *Jadid al Islam*, p. 178.

108 For the siege's length of time, see Garji, *Korot Zemanim*, p. 12. For the restriction to Herat's "walled section," called "the Mosallah," see Patai, *Jadid al Islam*, p. 178.

109 Patai, *Jadid al Islam*, p. 178; Nissimi, *The Crypto-Jewish Mashadis*, p. 28.

110 Garji, *Korot Zemanim*, p. 12.

111 Patai, *Jadid al Islam*, p. 178.

112 Ibid.

113 Nissimi, *The Crypto-Jewish Mashadis*, p. 62.

114 Ibid.

115 Ibid.

116 Yehoshua Raz, *Mi-nidhei Yisrael*, p. 434.

117 John R. Perry, "Forced Migration in Iran during the Seventeenth and Eighteenth Centuries," *Iranian Studies* Vol. 8, No. 4 (1975), pp. 209–210.

118 Excerpts from interview with a Jewish couple from Herat, January 2008.

CHAPTER 2

1 Pinhas Sadeh, *Jewish Folktales*, trans. Hillel Halkin (New York: Doubleday, 1989), p. 191. For the folktale's Afghan Jewish origins, see p. 433.

2 This seems to be reminiscent of the biblical story when Moses's staff changes into a serpent and back to a staff before Pharaoh (Exodus 7:10–7:20), much like the precious stones in "A Treasure from Heaven" change into a snake and then back into jewels.

3 "Afghanistan," *Encyclopedia Britannica* (2008).

4 *American Jewish Year Book* [hereafter, *AJYB*] 18 (1916–1917), p. 276; *AJYB* 23 (1921–1922); and *AJYB* 31 (1929–1930), p. 46.

5 Beginning in 1931, *AJYB* reported that 5,000 Jews lived in Afghanistan; see *AJYB* 32 (1930–1931), p. 229. According to *AJYB*, the population fell to 3,500 Jews in 1950 and grew in 1953 to 4,000 Jews; see *AJYB* 52 (1951), p. 199, and *AJYB* 55 (1954), p. 160. The number 4,000 in *AJYB* then stayed constant for almost a decade until 1961; see *AJYB* 63 (1962), p. 491.

6 *AJYB* 64 (1963), p. 427; *AJYB* 67 (1966), p. 474.

7 Brauer, "The Jews of Afghanistan," p. 134.

8 Nehemiah Robinson, "Persia and Afghanistan and Their Jewish Communities" (New York: Institute of Jewish Affairs, World Jewish Congress, 1953), p. 28.

9 See Chapter 3 of this book for more on Jewish emigration from Afghanistan.

10 *AJYB* 18 (1916–1917), p. 276.

11 Hayyim J. Cohen, *The Jews of the Middle East: 1860–1972* (Jerusalem: Keter Press, 1973), p. 69.

12 *AJYB* 50 (1948–1949), p. 695.

13 Cohen, *The Jews of the Middle East*, p. 69.

14 Robinson, "Persia and Afghanistan," p. 16.

15 *AJYB* 52 (1951), p. 199.

16 Interview with a Jewish couple from Herat, January 2008.

17 Interview with a Jewish couple from Kabul, December 2007.

18 One interviewee from Herat explained, "For Rosh Hashanah and Yom Kippur, everyone had to bring their own sheep into the house, to make *shehitah* [ritual slaughter]. Everyone had his own sheep, their own meat. And the women, they do all these *bedikot* [checks] of the sheep—not the butcher." Excerpt from interview with a Jewish couple from Herat, January 2008.

19 Nissimi, *The Crypto-Jewish Mashadis*, pp. 27–28.

20 Interview with a Jewish man from Kabul (1), August 2007.

21 Cohen, *Jews of the Middle East*, p. 166.

22 Ida Cowen, *Jews in Remote Corners of the World* (New Jersey: Prentice Hall Inc., 1971), p. 246.

23 Ibid.

24 Brauer, "The Jews of Afghanistan," p. 122.

25 Cowen, *Jews in Remote Corners*, pp. 131–132.

26 Interviews with a Jewish man from Kabul, August 2007 (1); with a Jewish couple from Kabul, December 2007; and with a Jewish couple from Herat, January 2008.

27 Brauer, "The Jews of Afghanistan," p. 134.

28 Ibid. 134–135.

29 Blady, *Jewish Communities*, p. 201.

30 Brauer, "The Jews of Afghanistan," p. 128.

31 Some Jews observe the practice of *kol isha* [voice of a woman], which forbids men to hear female voices in certain contexts, such as singing. Commentators differ over the parameters and applications of *kol isha*. See Berakhot 24a and Kiddushin 70a.

32 Brauer, "The Jews of Afghanistan," pp. 130–131. For more on marriage rites of the Jews in Afghanistan, see ibid. 128–129, and Ben Yoseff, ed., *Brides and Betrothals*.

33 Brauer, "The Jews of Afghanistan," p. 134.

34 Cohen, *Jews of the Middle East*, p. 246.

35 "Afghanistan," *Encyclopedia Britannica* (2008).

36 Brauer, "The Jews of Afghanistan," p. 131.

37 Interview with a Jewish couple from Herat, January 2008. Interviewees detailed how Jewish women did not cover their faces in their homes or in the Jewish quarter.

38 Brauer, "The Jews of Afghanistan," p. 128.

39 "Dowry," *Encyclopedia Britannica* (2008).

40 The phrase *avodot parekh* is used in Exodus to describe the harsh labor of the Children of Israel in Egypt under Pharoah (Exodus 1:13–1:14).

41 Excerpt from an Afghan Jew's unpublished memoir, written in Jerusalem in 1987. He was born and raised in Herat. He wrote the memoir in Hebrew using Judeo-Persian "Rashi" script. For more on this script, see Chapter 2.

42 Gregorian, *The Emergence of Modern Afghanistan*, p. 315. Also see Hauner, *India in Axis Strategy*, p. 86.

43 Brauer, "The Jews of Afghanistan," pp. 123–124; Kashani, *The Jews of Afghanistan* [English], pp. 10–12.

44 "Jewish Settlers in Afghanistan," *The Jewish Chronicle*, January 16, 1914.

45 Kashani, *The Jews of Afghanistan* [English], p. 11.

46 Brauer, "The Jews of Afghanistan," p. 123.

47 Excerpt from interview with a Jewish man from Kabul (1), August 2007.

48 Kashani, *The Jews of Afghanistan* [English], p. 10.

49 Brauer, "The Jews of Afghanistan," pp. 123–124.

50 Kashani, *The Jews of Afghanistan* [English], p. 10.

51 Ibid. 31.

52 Interview with a Jewish couple from Herat, January 2008. They described how prayer books were mailed from Palestine to Afghanistan. It is unclear when these shipments started. For further discussion of the significance of Afghan Jews praying in the *Edot Ha-mizrah* version, see Chapter 4 of this book.

53 Cowen, *Jews in Remote Corners*, p. 246.

54 "The Last of the Lost," *The Jewish Chronicle*, February 8, 2002.

55 Zohar Hanegbi and Bracha Yaniv, *Afghanistan: The Synagogue and the Jewish Home* (Jerusalem: The Hebrew University of Jerusalem, 1991), p. 18.

56 Interview with a Jewish couple from Herat, January 2008.

57 Interviews with a Jewish man from Kabul (1), August 2007; with a Jewish man from Kabul (2), August 2007; and with a Jewish couple from Kabul, December 2007.

58 Cowen, *Jews in Remote Corners*, p. 237.

59 Ibid. 236.

60 See later in this chapter for a description of the 1920 *shaliah* [emissary of Zion] from Palestine to Afghanistan. Interviewees from Kabul said that the Lubavitch visitor in 1965 was the only *shaliah* in Afghanistan during their lifetimes. Interview with a Jewish couple from Kabul, December 2007.

61 Cowen, *Jews in Remote Corners*, p. 237.

62 Excerpt from interview with a Jewish man from Kabul (1), August 2007.

63 Brauer, "The Jews of Afghanistan," p. 135.

64 Interviewees from Herat detailed the names of the synagogues there; interview with a Jewish couple from Herat, January 2008. Also see Hanegbi and Yaniv, *Afghanistan: The Synagogue and the Jewish Home*, p. 18.

65 Interviews with a Jewish couple from Herat, January 2008; and with a Jewish couple from Kabul, December 2007.

66 Brauer, "The Jews of Afghanistan," p. 132.

67 Interviews with a Jewish man from Kabul (1), August 2007; with a Jewish man from Kabul (2), August 2007; with a Jewish couple from Kabul, December 2007; and with a Jewish couple from Herat, January 2008. Interviewees from Herat and Kabul described the synagogues' women's sections.

68 Hanegbi and Yaniv, *Afghanistan: The Synagogue and the Jewish Home*, p. 18. Also see pp. 60–65 for photos of synagogues in Afghanistan.

69 Interviews with a Jewish man from Kabul (1), August 2007; and with a Jewish couple from Kabul, December 2007.

70 Interviews with a Jewish couple from Kabul, December 2007; and with a Jewish couple from Herat, January 2008.

71 Cowen, *Jews in Remote Corners*, p. 243.

72 Hanegbi and Yaniv, *Afghanistan: The Synagogue and the Jewish Home*, p. 31.

73 Cowen, *Jews in Remote Corners*, p. 243.

74 Interviews with a Jewish man from Kabul (1), August 2007; with a Jewish man from Kabul (2), August 2007; with a Jewish couple from Kabul, December 2007; and with a Jewish couple from Herat, January 2008.

75 Brauer, "The Jews of Afghanistan," p. 133; Yehoshua Raz, *Mi-nidhei Yisrael*, p. 434.

76 Interviews with a Jewish man from Kabul (1), August 2007; with a Jewish man from Kabul (2), August 2007; with a Jewish couple from Kabul, December 2007; and with a Jewish couple from Herat, January 2008.

77 Many interviewees expressed their affection for *Ein Yaakov*. Interviews with a Jewish man from Kabul (1), August 2007; with a Jewish man from Kabul (2), August 2007; with a Jewish couple from Kabul, December 2007; and with a Jewish couple from Herat, January 2008.

78 Yehoshua Raz, *Mi-nidhei Yisrael*, p. 436.

79 Interviews with a Jewish couple from Kabul, December 2007; and with a Jewish couple from Herat, January 2008. Also see Brauer, "The Jews of Afghanistan," p. 133.

80 Finkelstein, *The Jews: Their History, Culture, and Tradition*, p. 1,177.

81 See this book's Photographs for a sample of Judeo-Persian script.

82 Interviews with a Jewish man from Kabul (2), August 2007; with a Jewish couple from Kabul, December 2007; and with a Jewish couple from Herat, January 2008.

83 Yehoshua Raz, *Mi-nidhei Yisrael*, p. 435.

84 Ibid. 444.

85 Ibid. 430.

86 Ibid. Today, in the 21st century, literacy rates in Afghanistan seem to have significantly improved in the past fifty or sixty years, but there are still large gains to be made. According to the website of the U.S. Central

Intelligence Agency in 2010, only about 50% of men and 12% of women in Afghanistan's general population are literate. See the "World Factbook: Afghanistan" on the website of the Central Intelligence Agency, May 27, 2010, accessed from https://www.cia.gov/library/publications/the-world-factbook/geos/af.html?sid=y419So.

87 Robinson, "Persia and Afghanistan," p. 26.

88 Yehoshua Raz, *Mi-nidhei Yisrael*, p. 431.

89 Cowen, *Jews in Remote Corners*, p. 239. Cowen, an American Jewish woman who traveled to Afghanistan in 1966/1967, describes how she sought out Jews in Herat by speaking some Hebrew words to strangers. Several Jewish men then approached her and they spoke to each other in Hebrew.

90 Abe Mor, *Fathers and Sons* (Tel Aviv: Hidekel Press Ltd., 2004), p. 153.

91 Interview with a Jewish man from Kabul (2), August 2007.

92 Yehoshua Raz, *Mi-nidhei Yisrael*, p. 443.

93 Ibid. 441.

94 Brauer, "The Jews of Afghanistan," p. 133; Yehoshua Raz, *Mi-nidhei Yisrael*, p. 440.

95 Brauer, "The Jews of Afghanistan," p. 133.

96 Interview with a Jewish couple from Kabul, December 2007.

97 Yehoshua Raz, *Mi-nidhei Yisrael*, p. 436 and p. 442.

98 Ibid. 442.

99 Fischel, "The Jews of Persia," p. 138; Simon R. Schwarzfuchs and Frances Malino, "Alliance Israélite Universelle, *Encyclopedia Judaica* 1 (2007), p. 674.

100 Cohen, *Jews of the Middle East*, p. 54.

101 Ibid. 143.

102 Ibid. 144–145.

103 Ibid. 165.

104 Ibid. Also see pp. 141–142. In 1873, the Alliance wanted to start a school in Iran. Once the Jews of Tehran heard of the Alliance's plans, "Immediately, the enthusiasm of young Jews in the city was aroused and they founded a small school with 55 pupils, where Torah, Talmud, English, French, Persian, Turkish, and Arabic were taught." Though the Jews sought an Alliance director from the school's inception, the Alliance failed to send them one until 1898 because of budgetary troubles and teacher shortages.

105 Fischel, "The Jews of Persia," p. 143.

106 Ibid. 145.

107 Cohen, *Jews of the Middle East*, p. 144.

108 Yehoshua Raz, *Mi-nidhei Yisrael*, p. 438.

109 Ibid.

110 Excerpt from interview with a Jewish couple from Herat, January 2008.

111 Personal communication to author from Rosanne Klass, former *New York Times* correspondent in Afghanistan, June 27, 2010.

112 Yehoshua Raz, *Mi-nidhei Yisrael*, p. 438.

113 Ibid.

114 Ibid.

115 Ibid. 438–439.

116 Ibid. 439.

117 Interview with a Jewish couple from Herat, January 2008. The couple, who left Afghanistan in 1956, said that no *shlihim* [emissaries of Zion] from the Land of Israel came to Afghanistan in general.

118 Brauer, "The Jews of Afghanistan," p. 133.

119 Yehoshua Raz, *Mi-nidhei Yisrael*, p. 440.

120 Interview with a Jewish man from Kabul (2), August 2007.

121 Interview with a Jewish couple from Herat, January 2008.

122 Ibid.

123 Interview with a Jewish couple from Kabul, December 2007.

124 Yehoshua Raz, *Mi-nidhei Yisrael*, p. 439.

125 Personal communication to author from Rosanne Klass, former *New York Times* correspondent in Afghanistan, June 27, 2010.

126 Interview with a Jewish couple from Kabul, December 2007.

127 Ibid.

128 Ibid.

129 For more on the opposition of Herat's Jewish community to entering Afghan public schools, see Cowen, *Jews in Remote Corners*, p. 249.

CHAPTER 3

1 Sadeh, *Jewish Folktales*, pp. 328–329. For the folktale's Afghan Jewish origins, see p. 440.

2 In her dissertation, Sara Beth Koplik also argues that discrimination against Afghan Jews was mostly present within the economic field. To date, her work is one of the most comprehensive studies of the causes behind Afghan Jewish emigration in the 20th century. See Sara Beth Koplik, "The Demise of the Jewish Community in Afghanistan, 1933–1954" (Ph.D. diss., University of London, 2003).

3 Bentzion Yehoshua, *Germanim, Natsim, Vi-sinat Yisrael Bi-afghanistan* [Germans, Nazis, and Anti-Semitism in Afghanistan] (Jerusalem: Rimon Publishers, 1986). Also, many Jews could not legally enter Palestine after the British restricted Jewish immigration there, and so they had to settle in other countries.

4 Excerpt from "Report of Bank Millie's Activities in 1344 [1965]" (Kabul: Bank Millie, 1345), in Maxwell J. Fry, *The Afghan Economy: Money, Finance and the Critical Constraints to Economic Development* (Leiden: E.J. Brill, 1974), p. 83.

5 Gregorian, *The Emergence of Modern Afghanistan*, p. 301.

6 Ibid. 314. Also see Fry, *The Afghan Economy*, pp. 83–85.

7 Gregorian, *The Emergence of Modern Afghanistan*, p. 363.

8 Ibid. 315. Also see Hauner, *India in Axis Strategy*, p. 86.

9 Craig Baxter, "Afghanistan: A Country Study," ed. Peter R. Blood

(GPO for Library of Congress, 1997), accessed from http://lcweb2.loc. gov/cgi-bin/query2/r?frd/cstdy:@field(DOCID+af0021). For more on the Anglo-Afghan wars, see Tanner, *Afghanistan*.

10 Excerpt from *Islah* [Newspaper in Kabul], July 8, 1931, in Gregorian, *The Emergence of Modern Afghanistan*, p. 321.

11 Gregorian, *The Emergence of Modern Afghanistan*, p. 322.

12 Ibid. 332–333.

13 Ibid. 322.

14 Ibid. 335.

15 Ibid. 337–338.

16 Baxter, "Afghanistan: A Country Study" (GPO for Library of Congress, 1997).

17 Hauner, *India in Axis Strategy*, p. 73; Hauner reports that 72 Germans came to Afghanistan in 1924.

18 Ibid. 53.

19 Ibid. 81.

20 United States Department of State, *Documents on German Foreign Policy, 1918–1945* [hereafter, DGFP], Series D (1937–1945): The War Years, Vol. VIII (Washington D.C.: United States Department of State, 1949), "Memorandum of the Aussenpolitisches Amt," December 18, 1939, p. 550.

21 Gregorian, *The Emergence of Modern Afghanistan*, p. 379.

22 DGFP, Series D, Vol. VIII, "Memorandum of the Aussenpolitisches Amt," December 18, 1939, p. 551.

23 Hauner, *India in Axis Strategy*, p. 77.

24 Gregorian, *The Emergence of Modern Afghanistan*, p. 380.

25 Hauner, *India in Axis Strategy*, p. 73.

26 Gregorian, *The Emergence of Modern Afghanistan*, p. 380.

27 Ibid.

28 Kashani, *The Jews of Afghanistan* [English], p. 22.

29 Central Zionist Archives [hereafter, CZA] F38/1129, "War Crimes Document: Affidavit of Expense Accounts for Hadj Amin El Husseini, Rashid Alu El Gilani [*sic*], Afghanistan Foreign Minister Ghulham Siddique and Others," from the Office of Chief of Counsel of War Crimes, October 1947.

30 DGFP, Series D, Vol. VIII, "Memorandum of the Aussenpolitisches Amt (Subject: Operation against India)," December 12, 1939, pp. 527–529.

31 Norman A. Stillman, *The Jews of Arab Lands in Modern Times* (Philadelphia: The Jewish Publication Society, 2003), p. 116.

32 Ibid. 117–119. During this state of transition, Iraqis attacked the Baghdadi Jewish community in a pogrom which the Jews called the "*Farhud.*" For more on the *Farhud*, which began on June 1, 1941, and killed over 150 Jews, see later in this chapter.

33 DGFP, Series D, Vol. XIII, "Memorandum by Minister Grobba," August 5, 1941, p. 286.

34 DGFP, Series D, Vol. XIII, "Memorandum by an Official of the Foreign

Minister's Secretariat (Record of the Conversation between the Fuhrer and the Grand Mufti of Jerusalem on November 28, 1941, in the Presence of the Reich Foreign Minister and Minister Grobba in Berlin)," November 30, 1941, p. 881.

35 On November 28, 1941, during a separate meeting with Reich Foreign Minister Ribbentrop before speaking with Hitler, the Grand Mufti "stressed the fact that the Arabs were naturally friends of Germany because both were fighting three common foes: the English, the Jews, and Bolshevism." See DGFP, Series D, Vol. XIII, "Memorandum by an Official of the Foreign Minister's Secretariat (Record of the Conversation of the Grand Mufti with the Foreign Minister in Berlin on November 28, 1941)," November 28, 1941, p. 876.

36 DGFP, Series D, Vol. XIII, "Memorandum by an Official of the Foreign Minister's Secretariat (Record of the Conversation between the Fuhrer and the Grand Mufti of Jerusalem)," November 30, 1941, pp. 882–883.

37 Jewish communities in certain Arab lands, such as Tunisia, suffered from a concerted Nazi effort to persecute Jewish populations. See Stillman, *The Jews of Arab Lands in Modern Times*, p. 130, citing "Rudolf Rahn's Report to Berlin" (December 24, 1942) in Michael Abitbol, *Les Juifs d'Afrique du Nord sous Vichy* (Paris, 1983), p. 192.

38 See DGFP, Series D: The War Years. In particular, see DGFP, Series D, Vol. VIII, "Memorandum of the Aussenpolitisches Amt (Subject: Operation Against India)," December 12, 1939, pp. 527–529; DGFP, Series D, Vol. VIII, "Memorandum of the Aussenpolitisches Amt," December 18, 1939, pp. 550–551; DGFP, Series D, Vol. XIII, "The Minister in Afghanistan [Pilger] to Foreign Minister [Ribbentrop]," July 31, 1942, pp. 269–271; and DGFP, Series D, Vol. XIII, "The Foreign Minister [Ribbentrop] to the Legation in Afghanistan," August 9, 1941, p. 301.

39 Gregorian, *The Emergence of Modern Afghanistan*, p. 346.

40 Ghubar, Mir Ghulam Muhammed, "Role of Afghanistan in the Civilization of Islam," *Afghanistan* (January–March 1946), pp. 26–32, in Gregorian, *The Emergence of Modern Afghanistan*, p. 345.

41 Gregorian, *The Emergence of Modern Afghanistan*, pp. 345–346.

42 Baxter, "Afghanistan: A Country Study" (GPO for Library of Congress, 1997).

43 DGFP, Series D, Vol. XIII, "The Minister in Afghanistan [Pilger] to Foreign Minister [Ribbentrop]," July 31, 1942, pp. 269–271.

44 Baxter, "Afghanistan: A Country Study" (GPO for Library of Congress, 1997).

45 DGFP, Series D, Vol. XIII, "The Foreign Minister [Ribbentrop] to the Legation in Afghanistan," August 9, 1941, p. 301.

46 Hauner, *India in Axis Strategy*, p. 324.

47 "The Jews of Afghanistan: By a Special Correspondent," *The Jewish Chronicle*, February 3, 1950; Robinson, "Persia and Afghanistan," p. 28.

48 Brauer, "The Jews of Afghanistan," p. 125.

49 Robinson, "Persia and Afghanistan," p. 29.

50 Gregorian, *The Emergence of Modern Afghanistan*, p. 315. Also see Hauner, *India in Axis Strategy*, p. 86.

51 CZA Z4/30092, "Letter from the Boukharian Jews' Association to the Joint Foreign Committee of the Board of Deputies of British Jews, requesting assistance for Jewish refugees in Persia and Afghanistan," September 25, 1933. Also see "The Jews of Afghanistan," *The Jewish Chronicle*; Yehoshua, *Germanim*, p. 15; and Brauer, "The Jews of Afghanistan," p. 122. Brauer incorrectly writes that the expulsion occurred in 1936, but his description of the expulsion and the move to inner cities is otherwise accurate.

52 "The Jews of Afghanistan," *The Jewish Chronicle*.

53 Cowen, *Jews in Remote Corners*, p. 232.

54 See Brauer, "The Jews of Afghanistan," p. 122.

55 CZA Z4/30092, "Letter from the Boukharian Jews' Association to the Joint Foreign Committee of the Board of Deputies of British Jews, requesting assistance for Jewish refugees in Persia and Afghanistan," September 25, 1933.

56 CZA Z4/30092, "Letter from the Boukharian Jews' Association to the Zionist Executive of the Jewish Agency in London," October 17, 1933.

57 CZA Z4/30092, "Letter to the Executive from Dr. L. Lauterbach, 'RE: Russian Refugees in Persia and Afghanistan,'" October 18, 1933.

58 Ibid.

59 For example, see CZA S1/4291, "Letter from the Jewish Agency's Immigration Department to Yoseff ben Yehya Elias, Kabul, confirming Immigration Certificate and visa to Palestine," from Writings in Relation to the Granting of Permissions for *Aliyah*, August 23, 1935; CZA S1/4291, "Letter from the Jewish Agency's Immigration Department to Abraham ben Yacob Kasab, Kabul, confirming Immigration Certificate and visa to Palestine," from Writings in Relation to the Granting of Permissions for *Aliyah*, August 23, 1935; and CZA S1/4291, "Letter from the Executive of the Jewish Agency to the Commissioner for Migration & Statistics, Acting Director, Department of Immigration, requesting the dispatch of Immigration Certificates to David Katan and family, and Sion ben Eliyahu," from Writings in Relation to the Granting of Permissions for *Aliyah*, February 1936 [exact date unknown].

60 Gregorian, *The Emergence of Modern Afghanistan*, p. 389.

61 Robinson, "Persia and Afghanistan," p. 28; Yehoshua, *Germanim*, p. 34.

62 "The Jews of Afghanistan," *The Jewish Chronicle*; Robinson, "Persia and Afghanistan," p. 28.

63 Yehoshua, *Germanim*, p. 34.

64 Yehoshua Raz, *Mi-nidhei Yisrael*, p. 439, n. 290.

65 Interview with a Jewish couple from Herat, January 2008.

66 Excerpt from an Afghan Jew's unpublished memoir, written in Jerusalem in the 1980s. He was born and raised in Herat. He wrote the memoir in

Hebrew using Judeo-Persian "Rashi" script. For more on this script, see Chapter 2.

67 Interview with a Jewish couple from Herat, January 2008.

68 Haim J. Cohen, "Afghanistan," *Encyclopedia Judaica*, p. 432.

69 "Memo: Jerusalem," *The Jewish Chronicle*, November 4, 1949; Robinson, "Persia and Afghanistan," p. 31; Cohen, "Afghanistan," p. 432.

70 DGFP, Series D, Vol. VIII, "Memorandum of the Aussenpolitisches Amt," December 18, 1939, p. 550.

71 For Nazi propaganda in the Middle East, see Stillman, *The Jews of Arab Lands in Modern Times*, pp. 104–107. Also see Bernard Lewis, *The Jews of Islam* (New Jersey: Princeton University Press, 1984), p. 188. For more on Nazi efforts in the Middle East, see Lukasz Hirszowicz, *The Third Reich and the Arab East* (Toronto: University of Toronto Press, 1966) and Jeffrey Herf, *Nazi Propaganda for the Arab World* (New Haven: Yale University Press, 2009).

72 Robinson, "Persia and Afghanistan," p. 31.

73 "Palestine Report," American Jewish Committee, October 2, 1947.

74 For more on early Afghan Jewish settlement in Palestine, see Kashani, *The Jews of Afghanistan* [English], pp. 18–19.

75 Interviews with a Jewish couple from Kabul, December 2007; and with a Jewish couple from Herat, January 2008.

76 "Report from Israel," American Jewish Committee, June/July 1948. Also see "The Jews of Afghanistan," *The Jewish Chronicle*.

77 *AJYB* 50 (1948–1949), p. 695; *AJYB* 70 (1969), p. 460.

78 Interview with a Jewish couple from Herat, January 2008.

79 *AJYB* 55 (1954), p. 160; *AJYB* 63 (1962), p. 491; *AJYB* 64 (1963), p. 427.

80 Cowen, *Jews in Remote Corners*, p. 231.

81 *AJYB* 67 (1966), p. 474; *AJYB* 74 (1973), p. 576; *AJYB* 75 (1974–1975), p. 565; *AJYB* 81 (1981), p. 287.

82 *AJYB* 82 (1982), pp. 277–290.

83 "The Last of the Lost," *The Jewish Chronicle*, February 2, 2002.

84 N.C. Aizenman, "Afghan Jew becomes Country's One and Only; A Single Death in Kabul Cuts Community in Half," *The Washington Post*, January 27, 2005; Tsur Shezaff, "A One-Man Community," *Yediot Aharonot*, May 12, 2007; Jason Motlagh, "The Last Jew in Afghanistan," *The San Francisco Chronicle*, September 2, 2007.

85 Cowen, *Jews in Remote Corners*, p. 231.

86 Interview with an American Jew who traveled to Afghanistan in 1971, November 2007.

87 Alliance Israélite Universelle Archives, Liban I.C.4., "Une bombe eclate dans le quartier juif de Saida sans causer de victims," *Le Jour* (July 16, 1938), translated into English and published in Stillman, *The Jews of Arab Lands in Modern Times*, pp. 390–391.

88 Stillman, *The Jews of Arab Lands in Modern Times*, pp. 111–139.

89 Ibid. 119.

90 Abd al-Yehoshua Razzaq al-Hasani, *al-Asrar al-Khafiyya fi Harakat al-Sana 1941 al-Taharruiyya*, July 8, 1941, translated into English and published in Stillman, *The Jews of Arab Lands in Modern Times*, p. 417. The report also says that only "110 Jews and Muslims" were killed. Stillman explains that the Iraqi government consciously wanted to shrink the (Jewish) death toll; see p. 417, n. 19, and p. 119, n. 13.
91 Public Records Office (London) FO 371/82478, "Law No. 1 of 1950 (Annexure to the Ordinance for the Cancellation of Iraqi Nationality, Law No. 62 of 1933)," published in Stillman, *The Jews of Arab Lands in Modern Times*, pp. 525–526.
92 Stillman, *The Jews of Arab Lands in Modern Times*, pp. 141–176.

CHAPTER 4

1 Sadeh, *Jewish Folktales*, pp. 305–306. For the Afghan Jewish origins of "The Lamp That Passed," see p. 438.
2 I specifically use the language of "acculturation" or "adaptation," rather than "assimilation," to describe Afghan Jews' transition to the United States. A community that "acculturates" or "adapts" to a new country will retain elements of the group's original customs, while communities that completely "assimilate" will lose their distinctiveness as they move toward one prevailing American culture. See Anthony Richmond, "Migration, Ethnicity, and Race Relations," for the definition of adaptation, and Virginia McLaughlin, *Immigration Reconsidered*, for the definition of assimilation, cited in Rogaia Mustafa Abusharaf, "Structural Adaptations in an Immigrant Muslim Congregation in New York," in *Gatherings in Diaspora: Religious Communities and the New Immigration*, eds. R. Stephen Warner and Judith G. Wittner (Philadelphia: Temple University Press, 1988), p. 250.
3 Email to author from Benjamin Phillips, the Cohen Center for Modern Jewish Studies at Brandeis University, January 25, 2008.
4 For example, see the "National Jewish Population Survey, 2000–01" (New York, N.Y.: United Jewish Communities, 2001), accessed from http://www.jewishdatabank.org; and the "Jewish Community Study of New York, 2002" (New York, N.Y.: United Jewish Communities, 2002), accessed from http://www.jewishdatabank.org.
5 "Hebrew Immigrant Aid Society Arrival Statistics: Refugees Resettled in the U.S., 1980–2002," accessed from http://www.hias.org.
6 Felicia R. Lee, "Coping, Afghan Jews Look Back in Sorrow," *New York Times*, December 30, 2001.
7 Krastev, Nikola, "U.S.: Afghan Jews Keep Traditions Alive Far from Home," Radio Free Europe/Radio Liberty, June 19, 2007, accessed from rferl.org/featuresarticleprint/2007.
8 Michael Reichel, *Persian American Jewry at a Crossroads: Will the Traditions Continue?* (New York: LV Press, 2004), p. 62.
9 Interviews with a Jewish man from Kabul (1), August 2007; with a

Jewish man from Kabul (2), August 2007; and with a Jewish couple from Kabul, December 2007. Interviewees detailed the founding of the synagogue.

10 Interviews with a Jewish man from Kabul (1), August 2007; with a Jewish man from Kabul (2), August 2007; and with a Jewish couple from Kabul, December 2007. Interviewees described how the synagogue hired a rabbi.

11 Interviews with a Jewish man from Kabul (1), August 2007; with a Jewish man from Kabul (2), August 2007; with a Jewish couple from Kabul, December 2007; and with a Jewish man born in Herat and raised in America, March 2008.

12 Interviews with a Jewish man from Kabul (1), August 2007; with a Jewish man from Kabul (2), August 2007; with a Jewish couple from Kabul, December 2007; and with a Jewish man born in Herat and raised in America, March 2008.

13 Interview with a Jewish man born in Herat and raised in America, March 2008.

14 Interviews with a Jewish man from Kabul (1), August 2007; with a Jewish man from Kabul (2), August 2007; with a Jewish couple from Kabul, December 2007; and with a Jewish man born in Herat and raised in America, March 2008.

15 Interviews with a Jewish man from Kabul (1), August 2007; and with a Jewish man born in Herat and raised in America, March 2008.

16 Certificate of Incorporation of Congregation Anshei Shalom, January 27, 1978; [First] Bylaws of Congregation Anshei Shalom, 1980; and Revised Bylaws of Congregation Anshei Shalom, 2002. A Jewish couple from Kabul described the upkeep of Afghanistan's synagogues; interview with a Jewish couple from Kabul, December 2007.

17 Certificate of Incorporation of Congregation Anshei Shalom, January 27, 1978. Also see New York State's Religious Corporations Law, accessed from http://www.law.justia.com.

18 Brauer, "The Jews of Afghanistan," pp. 134–135.

19 For example, see the 1968 constitution of Northern Hills Synagogue, Congregation B'nai Avraham, of Cincinnati, Ohio in Daniel J. Elazar, Jonathan D. Sarna, and Rela G. Monsoon, eds., *A Double Bond: The Constitutional Documents of American Jewry* (Maryland: United Press of America, Inc.: 1992), p. 203. This constitution states, "A delinquent member . . . who is in arrears in the payment of dues for a period of six months . . . will be suspended from membership in the Congregation."

20 [First] Bylaws of Congregation Anshei Shalom, 1980; and Revised Bylaws of Congregation Anshei Shalom, 2002.

21 Interviewees described women's participation in synagogues in Afghanistan and New York. Interviews with a Jewish man from Kabul (1), August 2007; with a Jewish man from Kabul (2), August 2007; with a Jewish couple from Kabul, December 2007; and with a Jewish man born in Herat and raised in America, March 2008.

22 Certificate of Incorporation of Congregation Anshei Shalom, January 27, 1978; [First] Bylaws of Congregation Anshei Shalom, 1980; and Revised Bylaws of Congregation Anshei Shalom, 2002.

23 See the published documents of numerous American Jewish synagogues in Elazar, Sarna, and Monsoon, eds., *A Double Bond*, pp. 103–225.

24 Abusharaf, "Structural Adaptations," pp. 235–236.

25 Interviews with a Jewish man from Kabul (1), August 2007; with a Jewish man from Kabul (2), August 2007; with a Jewish couple from Kabul, December 2007; and with a Jewish couple from Herat, January 2008.

26 Interview with a Jewish couple from Kabul, December 2007. See later in this chapter for a discussion of some Afghan Jews' (Ashkenazi) pronunciation of the Sabbath as "Shabbos."

27 See Chapter 2 for more on the low rates of intermarriage in Afghanistan.

28 Interview with a Jewish couple from Herat, January 2008.

29 Certificate of Incorporation of Congregation Anshei Shalom, January 27, 1978; [First] Bylaws of Congregation Anshei Shalom, 1980; and Revised Bylaws of Congregation Anshei Shalom, 2002.

30 See Chapter 2 for more on Jewish education in Afghanistan.

31 Interview with a Jewish man from Kabul (2), August 2007.

32 Interview with a Jewish couple from Kabul, December 2007.

33 Interviews with a Jewish man from Kabul (1), August 2007; with a Jewish man from Kabul (2), August 2007; with a Jewish couple from Kabul, December 2007; and with a Jewish couple from Herat, January 2008.

34 Shoshana Feher, "From the Rivers of Babylon to the Valley of Los Angeles: The Exodus and Adaptation of Iranian Jews," in *Gatherings in Diaspora*, eds. R. Stephen Warner and Judith G. Wittner, p. 87.

35 Reichel, *Persian American Jewry at a Crossroads*, p. 66.

36 Ibid. 115.

37 Interview with a Jewish couple from Herat, January 2008.

38 Interview with a Jewish couple from Kabul, December 2007.

39 For more on Ashkenazi Jewry, see "Ashkenaz," *Encyclopedia Judaica* 2 (2007), pp. 569–571.

40 See Chapter 2 for more on Jewish religious observance in Afghanistan.

41 Certificate of Incorporation of Congregation Anshei Shalom, January 27, 1978; and [First] Bylaws of Congregation Anshei Shalom, 1980.

42 For more, see Louis Rabinowitz, "Shulhan Arukh," *Encyclopedia Judaica* 18 (2007), pp. 529–530.

43 [First] Bylaws of Congregation Anshei Shalom, 1980.

44 Revised Bylaws of Congregation Anshei Shalom, 2002.

45 Interview with a Jewish couple from Kabul, December 2007.

46 Ibid. For the stance of the Conservative movement regarding driving on the Sabbath, see "Riding to the Synagogue on Shabbat," *Proceedings of the Rabbinical Assembly* 14 (1950), pp. 112–188, accessed from http://www.responsafortoday.com. The Committee on Jewish Law and Standards proclaimed that one who lives a far distance from a synagogue

is "allowed to ride to the synagogue and back on Shabbat on condition that he will make no stops on the way. The minority ruled that in general it is forbidden to ride to the synagogue on Shabbat except for emergency situations, in which the individual will have to decide for himself."

47 For these documents of the Jewish Center, the Leo Baeck Temple, Northern Hills Synagogue, Congregation B'nai Avraham, and Kehillath Jeshurun, see Elazar, Sarna, and Monsoon, eds., *A Double Bond*, pp. 197–212.

48 Sarina Roffe, "The Term 'Sephardic Jew'" (date unknown), accessed from http://www.americansephardifederation.org.

49 Revised Bylaws of Congregation Anshei Shalom, 2002.

50 [First] Bylaws of Congregation Anshei Shalom, 1980; and Revised Bylaws of Congregation Anshei Shalom, 2002.

51 Interview with a Jewish man from Kabul (1), August 2007.

52 "Youth" interview (1), January 2008: with a female Jewish teenager born in America of Afghan-Jewish descent on her father's side.

53 Interview with a Jewish couple from Kabul, December 2007.

54 Ibid.

55 Interview with a Jewish man from Kabul (2), August 2007.

56 Interview with a Jewish couple from Kabul, December 2007.

57 Personal communication from David E. R. Dangoor, president of the American Sephardi Federation, July 2007.

58 Interview with a Jewish couple from Kabul, December 2007.

59 The number of non-Ashkenazi Jews in the United States was provided by the American Sephardi Federation; email to author from the American Sephardi Federation, October 7, 2009. For the number of all Jews living in America, the National Jewish Population Survey of 2000–2001 reports a total of 5.2 million Jews in the United States, while *AJYB* 107 (2007), p. 134, records a larger total of 6.4 million. Also see *AJYB* 107 (2007), p. 159–160, Table 1, for the number of American Jews in each state and how *AJYB* calculated 6.4 million Jews in the United States.

60 *AJYB* 107 (2007), pp. 133–134.

61 For a list of non-Ashkenazi synagogues, see "World Directory of Sephardic Congregations, United States of America" from the American Sephardi Federation, accessed from http://www.americansephardifederation.org. The percentage of non-Ashkenazi synagogues in America was provided by Dr. Jonathan D. Sarna, Joseph H. and Belle R. Braun Professor of American Jewish History at Brandeis University; email to author from Dr. Jonathan D. Sarna, December 5, 2005.

62 Marc Angel, *Seeking Good, Seeking Peace* (New Jersey: KTAV Publishing House, Inc.: 1994), p. 178.

63 "Youth" interview (1), January 2008: with a female Jewish teenager born in America of Afghan-Jewish descent on her father's side; and "Youth" interview (2), January 2008: with a male Jewish teenager born in America of Egyptian and Syrian descent. He attends the Afghan synagogue in New York, Congregation Anshei Shalom, even though his family does not come from Afghanistan.

64 Jonathan D. Sarna, "From Immigrants to Ethnics: Toward a New Theory of 'Ethnicization,'" *Ethnicity* 5 (1978), pp. 370–375.

65 Ibid.

66 Ibid. 374. Other examples include "social discrimination" and "immigrant restriction."

67 My thanks and appreciation to Dr. Sylvia Barack Fishman, Professor of Near Eastern and Judaic Studies at Brandeis University, for her guidance regarding the Jews' use of the *Edot Ha-mizrah nusah* while in Afghanistan.

68 Feher, "From the Rivers of Babylon to the Valleys of Los Angeles," p. 89.

69 Ibid 73.

70 Ibid. 74.

71 Hilda Nissimi, "Communalization of Memory in an Immigrant Community: The Mashadis after Mashad," *Modern Judaism* Vol. 26, No. 2 (2006), p. 157.

72 In contrast to Iranian Jewry after 1979, repatriation occasionally occurred among early twentieth-century European and Russian Jewish immigrants to America. For more on Jewish repatriation to Europe and Russia, see Jonathan D. Sarna, "The Myth of No Return: Jewish Return Migration to Eastern Europe, 1881–1914," *American Jewish History* Vol. 71, No. 2 (1981), pp. 256–268.

73 Interview with a Jewish man from Kabul (1), August 2007.

74 Feher, "From the Rivers of Babylon to the Valleys of Los Angeles," pp. 74–75.

75 For more on Iranian Jews in America and Jewish education, see Reichel, *Persian American Jewry at a Crossroads*. The author explains that he is the principal of North Shore Hebrew Academy, a Jewish day school in Long Island, New York, with a large Iranian student body.

76 Feher, "From the Rivers of Babylon to the Valleys of Los Angeles," p. 85.

77 Reichel, *Persian American Jewry at a Crossroads*, pp. 69–70; for more on Meshedi Jews' communal memory of the 1839 forced conversions, see Nissimi, "Communalization of Memory," p. 150.

78 Reichel, *Persian American Jewry at a Crossroads*, p. 80; Feher, "From the Rivers of Babylon to the Valleys of Los Angeles," pp. 74–75.

79 Interview with a Jewish couple from Kabul, December 2007.

80 Reichel, *Persian American Jewry at a Crossroads*.

81 Interviews with a Jewish man from Kabul (1), August 2007; with a Jewish man from Kabul (2), August 2007; with a Jewish couple from Kabul, December 2007; and with a Jewish couple from Herat, January 2008.

82 Reichel, *Persian American Jewry at a Crossroads*, pp. 88–89. The author sent 600 questionnaires to Persian Jews in Great Neck and received 142 in return. Percentages were computed based upon the 142 responses. The author found that the "average age of the respondents was 44.88 years; average residence in the United States was 23.06 years."

83 Nissimi, "Communalization of Memory," p. 159.

84 Interview with a Jewish couple from Herat, January 2008.

AFGHAN JEWRY PAST AND PRESENT

1 Tsur Shezaff, "A One-Man Community," *Yediot Aharonot*, May 12, 2007.
2 The restoration project as a whole started in 2002 in Kabul, but the restoration in Herat only began in 2005. See the "Aga Khan Trust for Culture's Project Brief on Afghanistan" (2008), accessed from the Aga Khan Trust for Culture's website, http://www.akdn.org/publications.asp ?tri=country&country=Afghanistan#Afghanistan.
3 Golnar Motevalli, "Relics of Old Afghanistan Reveal Jewish Past," Reuters, June 24, 2009.
4 Ibid. The article describes the restoration of the "Yu Aw" synagogue, which is Herat's "(Mullah) Yoav" synagogue.
5 Ibid.
6 Olaf Caroe, *The Pathans: 550 BC–AD 1957* (New York: St. Martin's Press, 1958), p. 4.
7 It appears that Afghan nationalists applied the Aryan-descent theory to *all* Muslims in Afghanistan. This stands in contrast to the legend of the Ten Lost Tribes, which circulated mostly among the Pashtuns. The Aryan-descent theory thus enabled Afghan nationalists to assert that their Muslim countrymen now shared the same ethnic origins in addition to the same religion. See Gregorian, *The Emergence of Modern Afghanistan*, pp. 345–346. The rise of the Aryan-descent theory in the 1930s coincided with—and seems to have been highly influenced by—the move of hundreds of Nazis to Afghanistan after it signed a series of economic treaties with the Third Reich. See Chapter 3 of this book.
8 Neumark, *Masah*, p. 99 [Hebrew].
9 Regarding the legend of the Ten Lost Tribes and Afghan Pashtuns, researchers in Israel launched a scientific study in 2009 to try to determine through blood sampling if the Pashtuns contain DNA characteristics that link them to Jews. See Amir Mizroch, "Are the Taliban Descendants of Ancient Israelites? Government Scholarship Awarded to Scientist Researching DNA Link with Remote Afghani Tribe," *The Jerusalem Post*, January 10, 2010. In another example, British researcher Theodore ("Tudor") Parfitt of the University of London has searched for evidence of the Ten Lost Tribes in South Africa; see Angus Shaw, "A Controversial Theory on Lost Tribe of Jews in Africa," *Los Angeles Times*, August 29, 2010.
10 "Afghanistan Digital Library Project at New York University, Spring 2003 Newsletter," accessed from http://www.nyu.edu/its/pubs/connect/spring03/afghan_library.html, citing Wasil Noor, "Chronological Survey of the Dari Books Published in Afghanistan," *Central Asia: Journal of Area Study* Vol. 1, No. 5 (Peshawar: Area Study Centre, University of Peshawar, 1980) pp. 78–156.
11 Interview with a Jewish couple from Herat, January 2008.
12 "Afghanistan's Untold Story: Stability, Tourists, Miniskirts," August 20, 2009, accessed from http://www.cnn.com. The article's interviewees also

said that their parents had separate dishes on which they served their Jewish neighbors. If this was true, it illustrates the openness between the Muslim and Jewish communities. But we should remember that Afghan Muslims tended to be warmer toward the Jews than vice versa. Many Jews somewhat feared the Muslim populace and the Afghan government, and did not actively try to mingle socially with non-Jews.

13 Reichel, *Persian American Jewry at a Crossroads,* p. 71.

14 Nitza Druyan, "Metamorphosis through Philanthropy: Yemenite Women in New York," *NASHIM: A Journal of Jewish Women's Studies and Gender Issues* 11 (2006), p. 108.

15 For example, see William Haller and Patricia Landolt, "The Transnational Dimensions of Identity Formation: Adult Children of Immigrants in Miami," *Ethnic and Racial Studies* Vol. 28, No. 6 (2005), p. 1,193. The authors describe the strong emotional ties of children of Latino immigrants in America to their parents' countries of origin.

BIBLIOGRAPHY

ARCHIVES AND PUBLISHED PRIMARY SOURCES

American Jewish Committee Digital Archive. Accessed from: http://www. ajcarchives.org/ajcarchiveDigitalArchive.aspx.

Center for Jewish History Archive and Library Collections, New York.

Central Zionist Archives, Jerusalem.
F38: War Crimes.
S1: Treasury of the Jewish Agency.
S6: Immigration Department of the Jewish Agency.
Z4: Jewish Agency Office in London.

Congregation Anshei Shalom, New York.
1) Certificate of Incorporation of Congregation Anshei Shalom, 1978.
2) [First] Bylaws of Congregation Anshei Shalom, 1980.
3) Revised Bylaws of Congregation Anshei Shalom, 2002.

Documents on German Foreign Policy, 1918–1945. Washington D.C.: United States Department of State, 1949.

Hebrew Immigrant Aid Society (HIAS) Digital Archive. Accessed from: http://www.hias.org.

"Jewish Community Study of New York, 2002." New York, N.Y.: United Jewish Communities, 2002. Accessed from: http://www.jewishdatabank.org.

"National Jewish Population Survey, 2000–01." New York, N.Y.: United Jewish Communities, 2001. Accessed from: http://www.jewishdatabank.org.

NEWS ARTICLES

"Afghanistan's Untold Story: Stability, Tourists, Miniskirts." CNN.com, August 20, 2009. Accessed from: http://www.cnn.com.

Aizenman, N.C. "Afghan Jew Becomes Country's One and Only; A Single Death in Kabul Cuts Community in Half." *The Washington Post*, January 27, 2005.

"Jewish Settlers in Afghanistan." *The Jewish Chronicle*, January 16, 1914.

Krastev, Nikola. "U.S.: Afghan Jews Keep Traditions Alive Far from Home." Radio Free Europe/Radio Liberty, June 19, 2007. Accessed from: http://www.rferl.org.

Lee, Felicia R. "Coping, Afghan Jews Look Back in Sorrow." *The New York Times*, December 30, 2001.

"Memo: Jerusalem." *The Jewish Chronicle*, November 4, 1949.

Mizroch, Amir. "Are the Taliban Descendants of Ancient Israelites? Government Scholarship Awarded to Scientist Researching DNA Link with Remote Afghani Tribe." *The Jerusalem Post*, January 10, 2010.

Motevalli, Golnar. "Relics of Old Afghanistan Reveal Jewish Past." Reuters, June 24, 2009.

Motlagh, Jason. "The Last Jew in Afghanistan." *The San Francisco Chronicle*, September 2, 2007.

Shaw, Angus. "A Controversial Theory on Lost Tribe of Jews in Africa." *The Los Angeles Times*, August 29, 2010.

Shezaff, Tsur. "A One-Man Community." *Yediot Aharonot*, May 12, 2007.

"The Jews of Afghanistan: By a Special Correspondent." *The Jewish Chronicle*, February 3, 1950.

"The Last of the Lost." *The Jewish Chronicle*, February 8, 2002.

SECONDARY SOURCES

Abusharaf, Rogaia Mustafa. "Structural Adaptations in an Immigrant Muslim Congregation in New York." In *Gatherings in Diaspora: Religious Communities and the New Immigration*, eds. R. Stephen Warner and Judith G. Wittner. Philadelphia: Temple University Press, 1988, pp. 235–261.

Adelson, Roger. *London and the Invention of the Middle East: Money, Power, and War, 1902–1922*. New Haven: Yale University Press, 1995.

Adler, Marcus Nathan. Introduction to *Massaot Shel R' Binyamin* [The Itinerary of Benjamin of Tudela] by Benjamin of Tudela. New York: Phillip Feldheim, Inc., 1907, xiii-xv.

———. Trans. "The Itinerary of Benjamin of Tudela." *The Jewish Quarterly Review* Vol. 18, No. 1. Philadelphia: University of Pennsylvania Press, 1905, pp. 84–101.

"Afghanistan Digital Library Project at New York University, Spring 2003 Newsletter." Accessed from: http://www.nyu.edu/its/pubs/connect/spring03/afghan_library.html.

American Jewish Year Book, Vols. 18–82. Accessed from: http://www.ajcarchives.org.

Angel, Marc. *Seeking Good, Seeking Peace*. New Jersey: KTAV Publishing House, Inc., 1994.

Asher, A., trans. "The Itinerary of Benjamin of Tudela." New York: Hakesheth Publishing Company, 1900.

Baxter, Craig. "Afghanistan: A Country Study." Ed. Peter R. Blood. GPO for

Library of Congress, 1997. Accessed from: http://lcweb2.loc.gov/cgibin/ query2/r?frd/cstdy:@field(DOCID+ af0021).

Benjamin II, J.J. *Eight Years in Asia and Africa: From 1846 to 1855*. Hanover: J.J. Benjamin II, 1859.

Ben-Tzvi, Isaac. *The Exiled and the Redeemed*. Philadelphia: The Jewish Publication Society of America, 1961.

Ben Yoseff, No'am Baraam, ed. *Brides and Betrothals: Jewish Wedding Rituals in Afghanistan*. Jerusalem: The Israel Museum, 1998.

Blady, Ken. *Jewish Communities in Exotic Places*. New Jersey: Jason Aronson, Inc., 2000.

Brauer, Erich. "The Jews of Afghanistan." *Jewish Social Studies* Vol. 4, No. 2 (1942), pp. 121–138.

Bruno, Andrea. "Notes on the Discovery of Hebrew Inscriptions in the Vicinity of the Minaret of Jam." *East and West (Rome)* 14 (1963), pp. 206–208.

Caroe, Olaf. *The Pathans: 550 BC–AD 1957*. New York: St. Martin's Press, 1958.

"Central Intelligence Agency: The World Factbook: Afghanistan." May 27, 2010. Accessed from: http://www.cia.gov/library/publications/theworldfact book/geos/af.html?sid=y419So.

Cohen, Hayyim J. *The Jews of the Middle East: 1860–1972*. Jerusalem: Keter Press, 1973.

Cohen, Michael. *Journey among Nations*. Colorado: Outskirts Press, 2007.

Cowen, Ida. *Jews in Remote Corners of the World*. New Jersey: Prentice Hall Inc., 1971.

Druyan, Nitza. "Metamorphosis through Philanthropy: Yemenite Women in New York." *NASHIM: A Journal of Jewish Women's Studies and Gender Issues* 11 (2006), pp. 105–125.

Elazar, Daniel J., Jonathan D. Sarna, and Rela G. Monsoon, eds. *A Double Bond: The Constitutional Documents of American Jewry*. Maryland: United Press of America, Inc., 1992.

Encyclopedia Britannica (2007) and (2008).

Encyclopedia Judaica (2007).

Encyclopedia of Islam, Second Edition (2010).

Encyclopedia of Islam and the Muslim World (2004).

Encyclopedia of the Modern Middle East and North Africa.

Feher, Shoshana. "From the Rivers of Babylon to the Valleys of Los Angeles: The Exodus and Adaptation of Iranian Jews." In *Gatherings in Diaspora: Religious Communities and the New Immigration*, eds. R. Stephen Warner and Judith G. Wittner. Philadelphia: Temple University Press, 1988, pp. 71–94.

Finkelstein, Louis, ed. *The Jews: Their History, Culture and Religion.* New York: Harper and Brothers, 1949.

Fischel, Walter J. "The Jews of Central Asia (Khorasan) in Medieval Hebrew and Islamic Literature." *Historia Judaica* 7 (1945), pp. 29–50.

———. "The Jews of Medieval Iran from the 16th to the 18th Centuries: Political, Economic, and Communal Aspects." *Irano-Judaica* I (1982), pp. 265–291.

———. "The Jews of Persia, 1795–1940." *Jewish Social Studies* 12 (1950), pp. 119–160.

———. "The Rediscovery of the Medieval Jewish Community at Firuzkuh in Central Afghanistan." *Journal of the American Oriental Society* Vol. 85, No. 2 (1965), pp. 148–153.

Freehof, Solomon B. "The Song of Songs: A General Suggestion." *The Jewish Quarterly Review* Vol. 39, No. 4 (1949), pp. 397–402.

Fry, Maxwell J. *The Afghan Economy: Money, Finance and the Critical Constraints to Economic Development.* Leiden: E.J. Brill, 1974.

Garji, Mattatya. *Korot Zemanim* [Chronicles of Afghanistan [*sic*] Jewry 1857–1904]. Jerusalem: Reuben Kashani, 1970.

Gregorian, Vartan. *The Emergence of Modern Afghanistan: Politics of Reform and Modernization, 1880–1946.* Stanford: Stanford University Press, 1969.

Haller, William and Patricia Landolt. "The Transnational Dimensions of Identity Formation: Adult Children of Immigrants in Miami." *Ethnic and Racial Studies* Vol. 28, No. 6 (2005), pp. 1,182–1,214.

Hanegbi, Zohar and Bracha Yaniv. *Afghanistan: The Synagogue and the Jewish Home.* Jerusalem: The Hebrew University of Jerusalem, 1991.

Hanifi, Muhammed Jamil. *Historical and Cultural Dictionary of Afghanistan.* Metuchen, New Jersey: Scarecrow Press, 1976.

Hauner, Milan. *India in Axis Strategy: Germany, Japan and Indian Nationalists in the Second World War.* Stuttgart, Germany: Klett-Cotta, 1981.

Henning, W.B. "The Inscriptions of Tang-I Azao." *Bulletin School of Oriental and African Studies* 20 (1957), pp. 335–342.

Herf, Jeffrey. *Nazi Propaganda for the Arab World.* New Haven: Yale University Press, 2009.

Hirszowicz, Lukasz. *The Third Reich and the Arab East.* Toronto: University of Toronto Press, 1966.

Kashani, Reuben. *Anusei Meshed* [The Crypto-Jews of Meshed]. Jerusalem: Reuben Kashani, 1979.

———. *The Jews of Afghanistan* [English translation]. Jerusalem: Reuben Kashani, 2002.

————. *Yehudei Afghanistan* [Hebrew]. Jerusalem: Reuben Kashani, 1975.

————. *Yehudei Paras, Bukhara, Vi-afghanistan* [The Jews of Iran, Bukhara, and Afghanistan]. Jerusalem: Reuben Kashani, 2001.

Keddie, Nikki R. *Qajar Iran and the Rise of Reza Khan: 1796–1925*. California: Mazda Publishers, 1999.

Klass, Rosanne. "In the Tents of Kabul." *Commentary* (October 2007), pp. 52–55.

————. *Land of the High Flags: Afghanistan When the Going Was Good*. Hong Kong: Odyssey Books and Guides, 1964.

Koplik, Sara Beth. "The Demise of the Jewish Community in Afghanistan, 1933–1954." Ph.D. diss., University of London, 2003.

Koppes, Clayton R. "Captain Mahan, General Gordon, and the Origins of the Term 'Middle East.'" *Middle Eastern Studies* Vol. 12, No. 1 (1976), pp. 95–98.

Kort, Zevulun, ed. *Bat Ha-melekh Shehafkha Li-ezer Prahim* [The Princess Who Became a Garland of Flowers]. Tel Aviv: Yehudit, 1967.

Lewis, Bernard. *The Jews of Islam*. New Jersey: Princeton University Press, 1984.

Mishael, Israel. *Bein Afghanistan Li-eretz Yisrael* [Between Afghanistan and the Land of Israel]. Jerusalem, 1981.

Mor, Abe. *Fathers and Sons*. Tel Aviv: Hidekel Press Ltd., 2004.

Neumark, Ephraim. *Masah Bi-eretz Ha-kedem: Suria, Kurdistan, Aram Naharayim, Paras Vi-asia Hamerkazit*. [Travel in the Eastern Land: Syria, Kurdistan, Iraq, Persia, and Central Asia]. Jerusalem: Epstein, 1860.

"New York State's Religious Corporations Law." Accessed from: http://www.law.justia.com.

Nissimi, Hilda. "Communalization of Memory in an Immigrant Community: The Mashadis after Mashad." *Modern Judaism* Vol. 26, No. 2. (2006), pp. 141–168.

————. *The Crypto-Jewish Mashadis: The Shaping of Religious and Communal Identity in Their Journey from Iran to New York*. Portland, Oregon: Sussex Academic Press, 2007.

Patai, Rafael. *Jadid al Islam*. Detroit: Wayne University Press, 1997.

Perry, John R. "Forced Migration in Iran during the Seventeenth and Eighteenth Centuries." *Iranian Studies* Vol. 8, No. 4 (1975), pp. 199–215.

"Project Brief on Afghanistan," the Aga Khan Trust for Culture, 2008 Accessed from: http://www.akdn.org/publications.asp?tri=country&count ry=Afghanistan#Afghanistan.

Rapp, Eugen. "The Judeo-Persian Hebrew Inscriptions of Afghanistan." *East and West (Rome)* 17 (1967), pp. 51–58.

Reichel, Michael. *Persian American Jewry at a Crossroads: Will the Traditions Continue?* New York: LV Press, 2004.

"Riding to the Synagogue on Shabbat," *Proceedings of the Rabbinical Assembly* 14 (1950), pp. 112–188. Accessed from: http://www.responsafortoday.com.

Robinson, Nehemiah. "Persia and Afghanistan and Their Jewish Communities." New York: Institute of Jewish Affairs, World Jewish Congress, 1953, pp. 15–31.

Roffe, Sarina. "The Term 'Sephardic Jew.'" (Date unknown). Accessed from: http://www.americansephardifederation.org.

Sadeh, Pinhas. *Jewish Folktales*. Trans. Hillel Halkin. New York: Doubleday, 1989.

Sarna, Jonathan D. *American Judaism*. New Haven: Yale University Press, 2004.

———. "From Immigrants to Ethnics: Toward a New Theory of 'Ethnicization.'" *Ethnicity* 5 (1978), pp. 370–375.

———. "The Myth of No Return: Jewish Return Migration to Eastern Europe, 1881–1914." *American Jewish History* Vol. 71, No. 2 (1981), pp. 256–268.

Sarshar, Houman, ed. *Esther's Children*. Philadelphia: The Jewish Publication Society, 2002.

Schwartz, Harold. *Miriam's Tambourine: Jewish Folktales from around the World*. New York: Seth Press, 1984.

Stillman, Norman A. *The Jews of Arab Lands: A History and Source Book*. Philadelphia: The Jewish Publication Society of America, 1979.

———. *The Jews of Arab Lands in Modern Times*. Philadelphia: The Jewish Publication Society of America, 2003.

Tanner, Stephen. *Afghanistan*. New York: Da Capo Press, 2002.

Wolff, Joseph. *Narrative of a Mission to Bokhara in the Years 1843–1845*. Edinburgh: William Blackwood and Sons, 1848.

———. *Research and Missionary Labours among the Jews, Muhammedans, and Other Sects*. Philadelphia: Orrin Rogers, 1837.

Yehoshua, Bentzion. *Germanim, Natsim, Vi-sinat Yisrael Bi-afghanistan* [Germans, Nazis, and Anti-Semitism in Afghanistan]. Jerusalem: Rimon Publishers, 1986.

Yehoshua Raz, Bentzion. *Mi-nidhei Yisrael Li-anusei Meshed Bi-iran* [From the Ten Lost Tribes of Israel to Meshed's Forced Converts in Iran]. Jerusalem: Bialik Institute, 1992.

INTERVIEWS

(Names have been withheld for confidentiality)

1) *August 1, 2007: Jewish man from Kabul (1)*. Born in Herat in 1931/1932. He and his family went to Kabul in 1935. He left Afghanistan in 1956 to go to India, where he went to college in Bombay and studied accounting. He went to Israel in 1963, and came to America in 1964.

2) *August 12, 2007: [A second] Jewish man from Kabul (2)*. Born in 1943, he left Afghanistan in 1954 to go to America, and returned to visit Afghanistan in 1964, 1966, and 1976. Father is Afghan and mother is Bukharian. His parents met while his father traveled to Bukhara for business. His father was involved in the construction process of a new synagogue built in Kabul in 1966, called Shaar-i-Nau, the name of the area in Kabul where it was located.

3) *November 29, 2007: American Jew who visited Afghanistan en route to the Soviet Union in December 1971 and stayed with Jews in Kabul*. A college-aged student, he wanted to help improve the books accessible to Soviet Jews. He flew from Tel Aviv to Tehran, and then spent a four-day journey traveling through Meshed, Herat, and Kandahar until he reached Kabul. He spent Hanukah in Kabul in a Jewish couple's home.

4) *December 31, 2007: Jewish couple from Kabul*. The husband was born around 1947, and left Afghanistan in 1965 for boarding school in England. He went to America in 1969. His family left Afghanistan for America in 1967. His wife (date of birth unknown) left Afghanistan in 1973 for Israel. Both received formal Jewish and secular education in Afghanistan. They attended *heder* in Kabul as well as public schools there run by the Afghan government, which required the attendance of the city's children in the 1960s.

5) *January 3, 2008: Jewish couple from Herat*. Both born in Herat in the mid- to late 1930s (dates of birth unknown). Both their families lived in Herat since the mid-1700s. They left Afghanistan together with their young son in 1956 for Israel. The husband then went to America first in 1960 and brought his family to America in 1962. Both the husband's and wife's grandfathers, as well as her father, traveled from Afghanistan to Palestine in the late 19th/early 20th century for the Jewish holidays. The journey took about one and a half years from their departure until their return; they went from Afghanistan to Peshawar, then to Beirut, and finally to Jerusalem. The wife's grandfather, (Mullah) Yaakov Simantov, was the chief rabbi of Herat. As an elderly man, Simantov ultimately decided to stay in Jerusalem after one of his journeys there to spend his remaining years in the Holy Land.

6) *January 12, 2008: "Youth" interviewee (1)*. Born in 1987 in the United States. Female Jewish teenager of Afghan-Jewish descent on her father's side.

7) *January 13, 2008: "Youth" interviewee (2)*. Born in 1987 in the United States. Male Jewish teenager of Syrian and Egyptian descent. He attends

the Afghan synagogue in New York, Congregation Anshei Shalom. His parents left their countries of origin for Israel, and then for America in the mid- to late 1970s.

8) *March 2008: Jewish man born in Herat and raised in America.* Born in Herat in 1954, and went to Israel with his family in 1956. The son of the interviewed couple from Herat (above, January 3, 2008). In 1962, at age eight, he, his mother, and his brother went to America to join the father, who had gone to America in 1960.

INDEX